DEATH ANXIETY

The Series in Health Psychology and Behavioral Medicine

Charles D. Spielberger, *Editor-in-Chief*

Chesney, Rosenman Anger and Hostility in Cardiovascular and Behavioral Disorders
Lonetto, Templer Death Anxiety

IN PREPARATION

Elias, Marshall Cardiovascular Disease and Behavior
Hobfoll Ecology of Stress
Morgan, Goldston Exercise and Mental Health
Pancheri, Zichelli Biorhythms and Stress in the Physiopathology of Reproduction

DEATH ANXIETY

Richard Lonetto
University of Guelph, Ontario, Canada

Donald I. Templer
California Professional School of Psychology–Fresno

HEMISPHERE PUBLISHING CORPORATION
A member of the Taylor & Francis Group

New York Washington Philadelphia London

DEATH ANXIETY

2 3 4 5 6 7 8 9 0 BRBR 8 9 8

This book was set in Times Roman by Hemisphere Publishing Corporation. The editors were Christine Flint Lowry and Elizabeth Maggiora; the production supervisor was Peggy M. Rote; and the typesetter was Sandra F. Watts. Braun-Brumfield, Inc. was printer and binder.

Library of Congress Cataloging-in-Publication Data

Lonetto, Richard.
Death anxiety.

(The Series in health psychology and behavioral medicine)
Bibliography: p.
Includes index.
1. Death—Psychological aspects. 2. Anxiety.
I. Templer, Donald I. II. Title. III. Series.
[DNLM: 1. Anxiety Disorders—psychology. 2. Attitude to Death. WM 172 L847d]
BF789.D4L65 1986 155.9'37 86-3114
ISBN 0-89116-554-1
ISSN 8756-467X

To our readers, students, and colleagues;

and especially to Dr. Charles Spielberger

for his continued support and interest in our work.

CONTENTS

PREFACE

It is our hope that this book will bring into focus the question of how the study of death anxiety can find a prominent place in the behavioral and social sciences. Given the profound influence of death anxiety in our lives, its relative absence from the theoretical and therapeutic literature is a situation that should be rectified.

We have endeavored to join together theoretical analyses and research on death anxiety that have been carried out at universities, hospitals, clinics, battlefields, and in different occupational and cultural settings. In this way, the many reactions of death anxiety can be seen as an emotional and intellectual barometer of periods of both calm and turbulent. By bringing together theory and practice, researchers can establish a framework that enables them to explore and understand the composition, dynamics, and idiosyncracies of death anxiety. Clinical practitioners also should be aware of these features of death anxiety, in order to better design and assess treatment, intervention, and follow-up procedures.

In the Introduction, we present our approach to examining this fundamental human anxiety. The specifics are to be found in Chapters 2 through 4. In Chapter 2 we discuss the *correlates of death anxiety*, that is, sex, age, religion, personality, and occupational and environmental factors. Although correlations are a well-accepted way of providing systematic evidence of the operations of a particular variable, the reader will see that death anxiety does not quite fit the mold of other forms of anxiety. The underlying *structure of death anxiety* is explored in Chapter 3, in which we consider in detail its components and their relative importance. The *imagery of death*, both cultural and personal, is discussed in Chapter 4, with emphasis on the linkage between these symbols and the components of death anxiety. This chapter looks through a window into the intraphysic and historical forces bonding anxiety to a variety of human experiences. With this as background, Chapter 5 covers a number of possible *intervention strategies* to control and reduce anxiety about death, how effective or ineffective these attempts are, and suggestions for change. We are on the threshold of understanding the rhythms of death anxiety, and the interventions discussed are one indication of our uncertainty in stepping over this boundary.

In Chapter 6, we offer our concluding thoughts concerning what death anxiety is and how it behaves. It is part of the course of our lives, ever present, but not always felt. It is not like other anxieties, and at the same time, it is a part of these other forms of anxiety, and of our reactions to loss and to change. Those readers who are interested in the specifics of the *assessment of death anxiety* can turn to the Appendix, where they will find normative, reliability, and validity data.

Physicians, nurses, and other health professionals who are confronted not only with patients' and families' reactions to dying and death, but also their own feelings, will find this book a valuable source of information. Psychotherapists, clinicians, counselors, and social workers will also find this book extremely useful. The information on the relationship between religiousity and death anxiety, for example, should be interesting and thought provoking to ministers and rabbis. On a wider scale, *Death Anxiety* can serve as a textbook and/or supplement for undergraduate, graduate, and professional courses dealing with crisis, loss, change, and lifespan development.

No book could be started, let alone completed, without the understanding and help of others. This single paragraph serves as a reminder of the process—the joys and the struggles. We would like to express our deep appreciation to Joanne Robinson, who combines rare and accurate typing skills with the ability to decipher our mispelled words; Ed and Rosalie Levine and their wonderful family, who provided a warm and hospitable environment to write; Dawn DeCunha who understands and somehow manages to cope with the changing moods of writer-psychologists; Inge Kauffman and Joan Ensher for their information gathering skills; and Rosa Smith for her linguistic talents.

Richard Lonetto
Donald I. Templer

DEATH ANXIETY

1

INTRODUCTION

> ***A rich man asked Sengai to write something for the continued prosperity of his family so that it might be treasured from generation to generation.***
>
> ***Sengai obtained a large sheet of paper and wrote: "Father dies, son dies, grandson dies."***
>
> ***The rich man became angry. "I asked you to write something for the happiness of my family! Why do you make such a joke at this?"***
>
> ***"No joke is intended," explained Sengai. "If before you yourself die your son should die, this would grieve you greatly. If your grandson should pass away before your son, both of you would be broken-hearted. If your family, generation after generation, passes away in the order I have named, it will be the natural course of life. I call this real prosperity."***
>
> (modified from a Sufi teaching story)

Freud (1918) maintained that the unconscious does not know death and that no person really believes in his or her own mortality. "Our own death is indeed unimaginable and when we make the attempt to image it, we can perceive that we really survive as spectators." Using everyday examples of how people avoid talking about death, Freud displayed his endorsement of the ancient advice that "If you would endure life, be prepared for death."

In "The Tale of Three Caskets," Freud (1925) attempted to relate mythology and folklore to the topic of death. In a number of these fairy tales, there is a choice (e.g., between three maidens, with the youngest being the fairest and the most desirable). It has been suggested that the three women were fates, with the youngest combining desirability along with the fate of death.

According to Freud (1920), "the aim of all life is death" and the general tendency for all living things to return to an earlier state finds its parallel in human psychodynamics. Such a death instinct presumably accounts for aggression, sadism, masochism, and repetitive behavior.

Freudians have held fast to the belief that death anxiety is a derived phenomenon having its roots in castration anxiety, separation anxiety, and fear of annihilation. Death has also been viewed within this context as a lover, a reunion with the mother, a separation from the mother, a punishment for aggression, and a punishment for incestuous wishes (Fenichel, 1945; Brodsky, 1959; McClelland, 1963; Greenberger, 1965).

Jung (1933, 1959) emphasized the value of beliefs about death and the integration of such beliefs into daily life. Jung felt that life is like a great parabola, beginning with birth and ending with death; the first half is therefore concerned with the preparation for life and the second half with the preparation for death.

In disagreement with Freud, Klein (1948) wrote that fear of death, rather than being derived from it, reinforces castration anxiety. She adopted the extreme position that death anxiety is the root of all anxiety (e.g., Brown, 1959), maintaining that paranoid disturbances in adults are founded upon a fear of disintegration and annihilation.

Fromm (1964) focused upon the "necrophiliac," or "lover of death," who is enamored of anything pertaining to death or decay, somewhat like to Freud's anal character, and feeling a fascination with such things as dirt, corpses, and disease. He is an emotionally cold person who is concerned with order, force, and remembrances of the past. Although, according to Fromm, all persons feel a certain degree of necrophilia mixed with "biophilia" or "love of life," men like Hitler and Stalin may be regarded as extreme necrophiliacs who had an unlimited capacity and willingness to kill.

Interpretations of the fear of death as one form of running away from life come from the work of Adler (1927). He suggested that some persons use the excuse of fear of death to forego all achievement. They feel that life is too short and that everything is in vain. In addition, Adler claimed that the seeking of consolation in religion can serve the same purpose.

It appears that psychiatrists and psychologists of an existential orientation have directed appreciable attention to the repression of death, while Viktor Frankl (1955) urged his patients to seek meaning in every facet of their lives, including suffering and death. Frankl stated that life has meaning only because of mortality and that "if man were immortal, each action could be postponed . . . indefinitely."

The truth of the matter is that for many years, the repression of death anxiety received more attention than death anxiety itself. This clinical emphasis on the defense mechanisms employed to cope with such anxiety seemed to expand even more after the publication of Zilboorg's (1943) work on the necessity of repressing death anxiety in order to achieve a normal existence.

When does repression become part of this existence? When death anxiety first appears? Studies of the development of conceptions of life and death in childhood present a cogent argument for placing the origins of death anxiety in the period of early childhood, in the form of separation anxiety (Nagy, 1948; Anthony, 1973). Very young children are far more seriously affected by separation, particularly from their mothers, than they are by death. For these children, death and life are interchangeable. As they see it, people simply go back and forth between the two. In the middle and later years of childhood, there is a marked preference for external and more adult interpretations of death, embracing its universality. Separation fears have now given way to fears of being taken away by an agent of death and of experiencing pain, burial, and life after death (Lonetto, 1980).

Death anxiety in one form or another appears to be with us throughout the adult and later years, carrying with it attitudes about mortality that may not be very different from those held in preadolescence. Given its endurance and tenacity, the probability is high that the repression of which Zilboorg spoke will break down. Disruptions related to these defensive failures can then quickly and even traumatically alter an otherwise untroubled life, permeating it with feelings of vague uneasiness, alienation, and hopelessness as well as distortions in the perception of time and of the self. The struggle with ideas about death and the emotional content they contain is a fundamental source of human anxiety (e.g., Brown, 1959).

Most, if not all, forms of anxiety are considered to have the ability to rise up out of or fall back into the unconscious. Death anxiety is not in this "buoyant ball" category. It is difficult to imagine death anxiety held in check by selective defenses, year after year, below the elusive boundary where the conscious fades into unconsciousness, or easily pushed into some dark and forgotten recess. Death anxiety may well be an elemental structure of the unconscious and possess the ability to move, with some freedom, into conscious awareness. In its periods of calm and serenity, death anxiety gives the impression of being absent; yet in these moments, curative effects resulting in self-integration can come about (Kelman, 1960; Schulz, 1978). In its displays of turbulence and destructiveness, death anxiety can manifest itself in pathological disorders, and we still have much to learn about its influence on neuroses and psychoses.

Theological, philosophical, and psychological perspectives have converged on the vision of death anxiety as being multidimensional in nature. Interestingly enough, statistical procedures have confirmed this consensus (see Chapter 3). This unitary thing we have incorrectly thought death anxiety to be turns out to be composed of from three to five independent components. The most consistently reported of these, which also account for the major share of the systematic shifts in death anxiety, are best described as:

1. Concern about both the cognitive and emotional impact of dying and death
2. Anticipation and fear of the physical alterations brought about by dying and death
3. Awareness of the finite time between birth and death and of the rapidity of its passage
4. Concern about the stress and pain accompanying illness, disease, and dying

Questions naturally arise with regard to limiting the scope of death anxiety to a specific number of components. However, the emergence of aspects of death anxiety in studies employing different subject groups of varying ages and backgrounds with a range of death-related experiences – in addition to different analytic techniques – strongly indicates that these four descriptive components represent source rather than surface dimensions of death anxiety. And it is apparent that each of these components, singly or in combination, determines the level of assessed death anxiety as well as the relationship of death anxiety to a wide assortment of variables (see Chapter 2). What is not as yet apparent is which components and what combinations produce distinctly different assessments and correlations. For example, is the midlife dilemma a behavioral indication of an acute and sharp rise in the "awareness of time" component relative to the others? Or have the others become somehow less important? We need to know if death-related experiences bear a direct or indirect relation to the underlying structure of death anxiety or whether they run parallel to changes in the map of these structures. We may even find ourselves arguing at this point for a reexamination of the relationship between death anxiety and other factors in order to justify the continued use of linear rather than nonlinear methods of analysis.

Methodological problems will no doubt be resolved,* but there are other concerns that have, for one reason or another, escaped investigation. What

*For our less methodologically inclined readers and to maintain the flow of ideas about death anxiety throughout our book, we have placed the details of the measurement of death anxiety in the Appendix.

does it mean to feel too much or too little anxiety about death? What, if any, combination of components is required to produce a level of death anxiety necessary to sustain personal existence? These questions determine, in part, the direction for future research, more specifically: (1) identification of those components of death anxiety that are differentially influenced by internal and external factors; (2) identification of components that are similarly influenced; (3) identification of those components that are resistant to change; and (4) examination of the variations in the components of death anxiety, along with related alterations in cognitions, emotions, and behaviors. Implicit in this regard is the assessment of death anxiety many times over the life span, ideally from early childhood on.

It is increasingly apparent that the major issues surrounding death anxiety have involved the measurement of change in some way, whether in terms of the effectiveness of intervention programs (see Chapter 5) or with respect to personal and environmental factors (see Chapters 2 and 4). In fact, we have seen changes, subtle though they may be, mirrored in the shifting of death imagery away from the macabre spectre of death to that of the gay deceiver or gentle comforter and the relationship of these images to anxiety about death (see Chapter 4). Perhaps, the changes we are trying to study are but a small segment of the historical cycle of death anxiety.

Does death anxiety come full circle in the later years; returning to its original form of separation anxiety? Or is death anxiety simply a disguised form of separation anxiety throughout our lives? Death anxiety contains reactions to change, and in all change there is separation and loss. The very components of death anxiety itself could be incorporated into the foundations of separation anxiety; since time, physical alteration, stress, and pain can act as barriers, creating the illusion of the segregation of events and feelings of isolation. At the same time, intellectual and emotional interactions can act to intensify or diminish these illusions and feelings. To take this discussion a necessary step further, the components of death anxiety can be used to establish the basis for all anxiety as they touch upon change, loss, and separation. In this way, death anxiety is clearly a fundamental human anxiety; while its components have joined together in such a way as to make it a distinctive form of anxiety.

Our concern now is: Can psychology accept and cope with the fundamental and unique properties of death anxiety as a central feature of the human condition?

2

CORRELATES OF DEATH ANXIETY

It is often stated that generalizations are dangerous. This is true: but only when it is true. Generalizations are useful, even essential, in certain situations, dangerous in others. To say: "Motorcars are dangerous" is useful for a child, for a period of his life. After that it may become a barrier to crossing the road. At that point other generalizations are supplied, to protect the child for a period or to carry it to a stage further towards learning.

A huge area of human life and thought requires the intelligent use of generalizations: which includes using them, modifying them, and superseding them.

(Idries Shah, *Reflections*, 1971, p. 15)

A variety of studies have focused on intergroup differences with respect to death anxiety and correlations of death anxiety with other variables. In isolation, these findings do not easily allow clear-cut inferences to be made. However, in this chapter, it will become apparent that the composite of these findings does permit meaningful, internally consistent, and interconnecting generalizations. Unless the death fear instrument is specified in this chapter, the Templer Death Anxiety Scale (DAS) was used in each study under consideration.

AGE, SEX, AND PARENTAL RESEMBLANCE

One of the important early death anxiety studies (Templer, Ruff, & Franks, 1971) evaluated the degree of death anxiety as a function of age and sex in diverse populations. This work also included information on family resemblance that has implications for death anxiety interventions and led to the development of a two-factor theory of anxiety about death (Templer, 1976).

Subjects were (1) residents of an upper-middle-class apartment building in metropolitan New Jersey (N = 283), ranging in age from 19 to 85 years (mean age = 48.8 years); (2) low-income aides in a New Jersey Neuropsychiatric Institute (N = 125), ranging in age from 18 to 61 years (mean age = 33.2 years); (3) heterogeneous psychiatric patients (N = 137) from 17 to 59 years of age (mean age = 38.1 years) at Western State Hospital at Hopkinsville, Kentucky (this group was included as research demonstrated that personality correlates of the DAS are different in normal and abnormal populations); and (4) students (N = 743) from 13 to 21 years of age (mean age = 15.8 years) in three high schools in and near Hopkinsville, Kentucky, a city with a population of approximately 25,000. The parents, 569 fathers and 702 mothers of these students, ranged in age from 31 to 74 years, with a mean age of 44.0 years, were also given the DAS so that the scores of the adolescents could be compared with those of middle-aged persons and for the purpose of determining the presence of any parent-adolescent DAS correlations.

It is evident from the data presented in Table 2.1 that there is no significant relationship between DAS scores and age for any group studied. In addition, examination of the scatter plots failed to reveal any nonlinear relationship.

For 223 father-son and 419 mother-daughter combinations, significant differences in mean DAS scores were absent. In fact, the mean DAS scores of parents and their child of the same sex were very similar (father = 5.67, son = 5.83; mother = 6.52, daughter = 6.79). In all the groups studied, females exhibited higher DAS scores than males. These differences were statistically significant ($p < .001$) for the apartment house residents, adolescents, and parents of adolescents.

The reasons for the higher DAS scores of females are not clear. However, it should be borne in mind that females have tended to score higher on most self-report measures of anxiety, distress, and maladjustment. Also, psychodynamically oriented clinicians have favored the position that females have more separation anxiety than males, and they trace death anxiety to separation anxiety. On a more general note, the greater degree of expressed death anxiety in females may be a product of a culture in which males have traditionally been expected to be brave, even to the point of dying for their country in battle.

The correlations between DAS scores of the various groups are presented in Table 2.2. Of interest here is that all the correlations are significant at the .001 level.

TABLE 2.1 Death Anxiety Scale and Age Means, Standard Deviations, and Product-Moment Correlations for Various Populations

Population	*N*	Mean age (SD)	Mean DAS (SD)	Age-DAS *r*
Apartment house residents				
Male	123	47.8 (15.0)	4.85 (2.88)	—.04
Female	160	49.6 (16.3)	6.11 (3.31)	—.07
Combined	263	48.8 (15.8)	5.57 (3.19)	—.05
Psychiatric aides				
Male	13	33.2 (15.9)	5.08 (2.25)	—.08
Female	112	33.2 (10.1)	6.33 (3.24)	—.03
Combined	115	33.2 (10.7)	6.24 (3.17)	—.04
Psychiatric patients				
Male	78	39.4 (11.1)	6.50 (3.55)	.09
Female	59	36.3 (12.5)	7.15 (3.72)	—.15
Combined	137	38.1 (11.8)	6.78 (3.62)	—.03
Adolescents				
Male	299	16.0 (1.4)	5.72 (3.07)	.01
Female	477	15.7 (1.2)	6.84 (3.21)	.03
Combined	743	15.8 (1.3)	6.39 (3.18)	.00
Parents of adolescents				
Male	569	46.0 (7.5)	5.74 (3.32)	.03
Female	702	42.3 (6.5)	6.43 (3.22)	.01
Combined	1271	44.0 (7.2)	6.12 (3.28)	.00

TABLE 2.2 Product-Moment Correlation Coefficients between Death Anxiety Scale Scores of Adolescents and Parents

	Fathers	Mothers
Sons	.51*	.39*
Daughters	.34*	.41*
Combined adolescents	.40*	.40*
Fathers		.59*

$^*p < .001$.

In none of the samples was there any demonstrated relationship between death anxiety and age. This is inconsistent with what is perhaps the "commonsense" view that the closer a person approaches the end of life, the more fearful of death he or she becomes. However, the finding is congruent with numerous clinical reports that the so-called defense mechanisms of denial and repression are used extensively as a means of coping with death anxiety across a large age range (i.e., Kübler-Ross, 1969; Weisman, 1972).

The DAS scores of both male and female adolescents correlated most highly with the score of the parent of the *same* sex. The Z-transformation procedure showed the difference to be significant, both with male ($t = 1.66$, $p < .05$) and female ($t = 3.31$, $p < .01$) adolescents. Furthermore, the highest correlation coefficient obtained was between parents ($r = .59$). This suggests that explanations based upon principles of learning better account for the observed parent-child correlations than explanations in terms of genetic similarities. The substantial correlation between DAS scores of parents indicates that death anxiety is far from being dependent largely upon early childhood experiences and basic personality structure.

Death anxiety seems not so much a fixed entity as a *state* that is sensitive to environmental events in general and, in particular, to the impact of intimate interpersonal relationships. The particularly high correspondence between husband and wife death anxieties may be a function of the proximity of this relationship and of shared life experiences. Such a conceptualization provides a potential basis for the treatment of pathological death anxiety by a broad-spectrum behavioral approach; that is, one stressing a combination of desensitization therapy for the specific reduction of the death anxiety per se together with the behavioral resolution of interpersonal family problems related to death and dying. If death anxiety can be learned, then it can be unlearned.

It is likely that interpersonal relationships in addition to those within a family context determine the degree of death anxiety. Perhaps friends, teachers, clergymen, military officers, colleagues, neighbors, and psychotherapists influence a person's degree of death anxiety more than has been recognized.

The findings of the Templer, Ruff, and Franks (1971) study have been well replicated. Husband-wife death anxiety correlations have been found by Lucas (1974), and by Koob and Davis (1977). College student-grandmother death anxiety resemblance was found by Hartshore (1979) and sibling resemblance by Kirby and Templer (1975).

The higher death anxiety of females has been repeatedly reported (Aday, 1984–1985; Arndt, 1982, Abdel-Khaleb, personal communication, 1985; Berman, 1973; Cole, 1978–1979; Devins, 1980–1981; Koob & Davis, 1977; Litman, 1979; Warren, 1981–1982; Lonetto, Mercer, Fleming,

Bunting, & Clare, 1980; Lucas, 1974; McDonald, 1976; Mulholland, 1980; Salter & Salter, 1976; Sanders, Poole, & Rivero, 1980; Devins, 1980–1981; Templer & Salter, 1979; Smith, 1977; Templer & Ruff, 1971; Templer, Ruff, & Franks, 1971; Sadowski, Davis, & Loftus-Vergari, 1979–1980; Chiappeta, Floyd, & McSeveney, 1976; Dunagin, 1981; Young & Daniels, 1980). In fact, gender may be one of the variables that most consistently relates to death anxiety, not only in North America but cross-culturally as well (i.e., McMordie and Kumar, 1983).

Gilliland (1982) found higher female DAS scores for a general population but very similar means for the sexes in a psychiatric population. He stated:

> *Similar findings were only reported in the literature twice before in contrast to a larger number of studies that report higher means for females. One of the two studies reported the same mean for both sexes focused on psychiatric patients who had attempted suicide (Tarter, Templer and Perley, 1974). Possibly, one could cautiously propose that equal death anxiety of the sexes is found in psychiatric populations. The other study reporting the same degree of death anxiety for males and females was with homosexual participants. Perhaps a broader generalization is that the sexes obtain very similar scores in atypical populations.*

The absence of any relationship between DAS score and age is the rule, although small inverse significant relationships have been reported (Blythe, 1981; Cole, 1978–1979; Kelly, 1979; Devins, 1979; Johnson, 1980; Lattanner & Hayslip, 1984–1985; Keller, Sherry, & Piotrowski, 1984; Handal, Peal, Napoli, & Austrin, 1984–1985; Kane & Hogan, 1985–1986; Whittenberg, 1980; Sadowski, Davis, & Loftus-Vergagi, 1979–1980; Salter & Salter, 1976; Schulz, 1978; Stevens, Cooper, & Thomas, 1980; Tate, 1980). Shusterman and Sechrest (1973) also reported an inverse relationship with the Collett-Lester Fear of Death Scale. An inverse relationship is more likely to be manifested when the researcher includes elderly subjects. In fact, one of the highest negative correlations (r = 0.31) was reported by Tate (1980) for elderly women (mean age = 71.52 years, SD = 12.56). It appears that additional years beyond the midlife translate into more time for reconciliation to the facts of death.

Neustadt (1982) employed the oldest subjects that the present authors are aware of in death anxiety research. The 37 persons, 10 males and 27 females, were nursing home residents who ranged in age from 66 to 99 years of age, with a mean of 86.7 years. Also, the mean DAS score of 2.86 is the lowest that has been reported. The fact that there was not a significant correlation between age and DAS score differs from the inverse relationships reported by Tate and others with somewhat younger participants.

Elderly persons with insomnia were found to have higher DAS scores than elderly persons without insomnia. However, DAS scores of college students with insomnia and those without insomnia did not differ (Wagner, Lorion, & Shipley, 1983). Perhaps sleep is realistically associated with death anxiety in the elderly, who may feel that they will not wake up in the morning. For most college-age persons, death is a distant concern, and the probability of not waking up the following morning is extremely small.

Only one significant positive correlation between age and death anxiety appears in the literature. Templer, Barthlow, Halcomb, Ruff, & Ayers (1979) reported a correlation of .25 between DAS and age for penitentiary inmates, with a mean age of 29.57 years (SD = 7.58). This is a group of men society has labeled "deviant" and deserving of neither the respect and love of their fellow humans nor rewards by God in an afterlife. Age can serve to intensify this predicament in the minds of men in prison. It is suggested that future research be carried out to determine whether positive correlations exist in other populations that are condemned and stigmatized by society. It is possible that systematic negative correlations could be found in populations leading lives regarded as exemplary (e.g., the clergy and those who give unselfishly to others).

All of the above studies have involved presumably predominantly heterosexual populations. However, Templer, Veleber, Lovita, Testa, and Knippers (1983–1984) investigated the three basic dimensions of the Templer, Ruff, and Franks (1971) study with 260 gays, 165 males and 95 females from 17 to 87 years of age, with a mean age of 28.16 years. The males and females had almost identical DAS means—5.84 and 5.85, respectively. This contrasts with the higher female mean of heterosexuals. However, the other findings are consistent with the research using heterosexual populations. The death anxiety resemblance of husband and wife has its parallel in the demonstrated death anxiety resemblance of gay lovers who live together. There was a zero-order correlation of DAS score with age. And the gay DAS mean is in the midrange of those reported for nonclinical populations (Templer & Ruff, 1971).

OTHER DEMOGRAPHIC VARIABLES

In regard to race, some studies have found blacks to have higher death anxiety, in particular, in comparison to whites (Myers, Wass, & Murphy, 1980; Young & Daniels, 1980; Cole, 1978–1979; Sanders, Poole, & Rivero, 1980); while others have reported no difference (Pandey & Templer, 1972;

Tate, 1980; Davis, Martin, Wilee, & Voorhees, 1978). An investigation of death anxiety among Mexican-Americans may prove fruitful. This burgeoning population in the southwestern states is said to have a "death culture" that focuses upon death as an omnipresent fact of life. Other cultural and subcultural comparisons (e.g., English-speaking and French-speaking Canadians) may be interesting as well.

One study found rural dwellers to have higher death anxiety than urban dwellers (Devins, 1980–1981); another found the opposite (Whittenberg, 1980). Marital status, parenthood, and number of children were reported by Cole (1978–1979) not to be associated with death anxiety. However, using Dickstein's Death Concern Scale, Morrison, Vanderwyst, Cocozza, and Dowling (1981–1982) reported that men and women who never married had greater death concerns than those who were married or widowed. Iammarino's (1975) research revealed that high school students living with one parent had greater death anxiety than those living with both parents. McDonald and Carroll (1981) found that only oldest children had higher death anxiety than later-born children and associated this difference with the greater need for achievement of the former.

Several studies have indicated death anxiety to be inversely related to income and educational level (Aday, 1984–1985; Berman & Hays, 1973; Cole, 1978–1979; Kinlaw & Dixon, 1980–1981; Schultz, 1978; Templer, Barthlow, Halcomb, Ruff, & Ayers, 1979; Bolt, 1978). Nevertheless, all of the significant relationships found have been small. It would appear that there is a slight tendency for the more advantaged members of society to score lower on the DAS. Being white, male, highly educated, from an intact family, with a good income and a higher IQ tends to be associated with lower death anxiety. As ironic as it may be, those who ostensibly have more to live for, have less fear of death. At issue here is the question of whether death anxiety could be a function of lack of education and perhaps be reduced by knowledge and the removal of superstition. In an even more highly speculative fashion, it could be argued that fear of death is somehow employed by the more privileged to oppress the less privileged members of society.

RELIGION

In searching for the correlates of death anxiety, religion would certainly appear to be a major area to explore. Almost all the religions of the world have something to say about death.

Templer and Dotson (1970) administered the DAS and a religious inventory to 213 undergraduates at Western Kentucky University. Table 2.3

TABLE 2.3 Mean DAS Score as a Function of Religion Inventory

Question	Answer checked	College student subjects			Religiously involved subjects			Psychiatric patient subjects		
		N	M	F	*N*	M	F	*N*	M	F
1. What is your religious belief system?	Catholic	22	5.73		7	3.57		35	6.14	
	Jewish	1	10.00					1	8.00	
	Protestant	180	6.25		276	3.99		204	6.80	
	Nonbeliever	2	7.00		2	8.00	1.47	10	7.70	
	Other	8	9.88	1.70	11	3.82		26	8.08	1.10
2. How strong is your attachment to the belief system checked above?	Strong	84	6.24		195	3.73		120	6.48	
	Moderate	110	6.41		67	4.70		96	6.99	
	Weak	19	6.53	0.15	5	4.80	14.47**	60	7.50	1.52
3. How frequently do you attend an organized service or church group of some sort?	At least once a week	104	6.38		228	3.86		77	6.51	
	At least once a month	47	6.28		25	5.32		28	6.12	
	Several times a year	37	6.46		9	2.77		61	7.28	
	Rarely or never	25	6.36	0.02	4	6.00	3.45*	106	7.08	0.93

4. Are you presently of the same religious affiliation in which you were brought up as a child?	Yes	175	6.49		168	3.89		169	6.52	
	No	38	5.76	1.51	95	4.25	1.05	59	7.58	3.64
5. Do you believe in a life after death?	Yes	166	6.25		240	3.78		220	6.86	
	No	6	5.67		4	6.75		38	7.29	
	Uncertain	41	7.05	1.46	23	5.83	8.19**	18	6.06	0.77
6. Is the most important aspect of religion the fact that it offers the possibility of a life after death?	Yes	98	6.61		64	4.08		200	7.17	
	No	113	6.15	1.17	196	4.01	0.03	76	6.07	4.87
7. Do you believe that the Bible should be interpreted literally?	Yes	81	6.81		93	3.20		213	6.92	
	No	128	6.12	2.55	158	4.48	13.11**	63	6.70	0.16
8. How is the strength of your religious conviction when compared to those of others?	Strong	74	6.29		218	3.71		98	6.52	
	About the same	114	6.39		37	5.05		123	6.75	
	Weak	21	6.00	0.15	7	7.57	10.47**	55	7.75	2.02

*Significant at .05 level.
**Significant at .01 level.

presents the mean DAS scores as a function of answer checked for each of the religion inventory questions. None of the *F*-ratios approached significance. The authors stated:

> *The absence of any significant relationship between DAS score and religious variables is inconsistent with the impressions of many persons in the mental health and religious professions. Again, "common sense" suggests that one's religious beliefs are among the most important determinants of the meaning and feeling that one attaches toward death. It is unexpected that, on the average, persons who differ with respect to a belief in an afterlife, fundamentalism, strength of conviction, and participation in church activities, have about the same level of death anxiety.*
>
> *There appears to be two explanations for the lack of relationships between death anxiety and religious variables. One is a "balancing" interpretation that would state; for example, that the non-believer, who does not have a hell to fear, also does not have a heaven to anticipate, so that his or her overall level of death anxiety is the same as the believer. A weakness in this perspective is that it would be unlikely that the opposing factors would exert almost equal force in all of the eight religious inventory items for which no significant differences were found.*
>
> *A more parsimonious explanation would be that religion is not an important determinant of death anxiety level, at least in most populations. Religious and philosophical values do not form the cornerstone of life for most people in our society. Instead, it is one facet of life which tends to be compartmentalized from other aspects of living. Religious belief does not have a tremendous impact upon the sex life, social life, work, or recreation of the average person, and it probably, in like manner, does not have a tremendous impact upon feelings concerning death.*

A second study (Templer, 1972b) determined whether the results would be different with subjects who are deeply involved religiously. The subjects chosen had participated in one of two interdenominational, predominantly Protestant evangelical retreats in the Midwest and the South in 1969. All 390 participants were sent the DAS and the same religion inventory used in the earlier research; 267 of them responded anonymously as requested (see Table 2.3). It is clear that the "more religious persons," in the traditional sense, have lower DAS scores. Those persons who have a strong attachment to their religious belief system, attend religious functions more frequently, are certain of a life after death, believe that the Bible should be interpreted literally, and judge the strength of their convictions to be strong compared to those of others have lower death anxiety. Consistent with these findings is the fact that, with the exception of Neustadt's work with very elderly persons, the DAS means, both for males (3.67) and females (4.21), were lower than in any other research in which the DAS was employed.

In a very interesting study, Wittkowski and Baumgartner (1977) administered the DAS and the Boos-Nunning questionnaire on religiousness to elderly Catholic Germans in a nursing home. The Boos-Nunning scale yields six scale scores: (1) "general religiousness" pertains to belief in a personal God, a sense of security and safety, and meaning of life; (2) "church communication and information" assesses one's ties to the religious community and personal contact with congregation members; (3) "marriage and sexual morality" assesses endorsement of traditional attitudes toward such matters as premarital sex, abortion, and family planning; (4) "belief in God" pertains to the assumption that God overshadows the national laws; (5) "public religious practice" has to do with confession, communion, and various religious services; and (6) "knowledge of the church," as the name implies, taps religious knowledge such as the number and meaning of the sacraments.

From the correlations in Table 2.4, the strength of belief and ties to other church members are more apparent than specific knowledge of dogma, attitudes towards morality, and frequency of attendance. This supports the findings described in Table 2.3, in which the items pertaining to strength of belief yielded the highest *F* ratios, suggesting that if one wishes to use the dichotomy "faith" versus "good works," the former is more closely associated with lower death anxiety.

TABLE 2.4 Correlation between DAS and Boos-Nunning Religiousness Factors

Scale	Correlation with DAS
1	—.316*
2	—.423*
3	—.112
4	—.425*
5	—.272*
6	—.096

*$p < .05$.

Other studies confirmed the negative relationship between death anxiety and degree of religious belief and/or practice. Young and Daniels (1980) found that born-again Christians had lower death anxiety than non-born-again Christians; Minean and Brush (1980–1981) reported a slight but significant inverse relationship between death anxiety and belief in an afterlife. Aday (1984–1985) found that persons who attended church more often had lower death anxiety. However, some studies have demonstrated little in the way of significant relationships (O'Rourke, 1976; Sullivan, 1977; Ochs, 1979; Blythe, 1981; Arndt, 1982). And Slezak (1980) and McMordie (1981) both reported a curvilinear relationship with persons of intermediate religious participation having higher death anxiety than both persons high and low on the religious dimension. These studies support the contention of Alexander and Adlerstein in 1958 that the "degree of certainty" may be a crucial variable. Nevertheless, it probably can be said that the most useful generalization is that religious people tend to have low death anxiety.

The question of whether death anxiety varies as a function of religious denomination is certainly an interesting one, but sufficient evidence to provide a definitive answer has not yet been accumulated. Rubenstein (1981) found that the Jewish adult children of Holocaust survivors did not differ from Jewish control subjects but that both groups had higher DAS scores than are ordinarily reported in nonclinical populations. He noted that previous research (Goodman, 1978) also found high DAS scores among Jewish Holocaust groups. Further research is needed to substantiate this possible phenomenon and the hypothesis that any differences could be related to belief in an afterlife. A recent study found that Jews are less likely than Christians to believe in a personal life after death (Dixon & Kinlaw, 1982–1983). On the other hand, Catholics, who traditionally are regarded as having at least as much belief in an afterlife as Protestants, were found in Northern Ireland to have greater death anxiety than Protestants (Mercer, Bunting, & Snook, 1979; Lonetto, Mercer, Fleming, Bunting, & Clare, 1980). Possibly, if the death anxiety of Jews is high, this is a function of their having for centuries suffered death at the hands of a multitude of persecutors.

The above studies relating death anxiety to religion have used subjects from populations presumed to be psychologically normal. It may or may not be possible on the basis of these studies to form generalizations applying to disturbed individuals. The religious inventory in Table 2.3 and the DAS were administered by Templer and Ruff (1975) to 276 psychiatric patients in a state hospital; 123 with a diagnosis of schizophrenia, 67 with alcohol addiction, 31 with organic brain syndrome, 12 with depressive neurosis, 10 with borderline or mild mental retardation, 9 with psychotic depressive reaction, 8 with manic-depressive illness, 7 with personality disorder, 3 with paranoid state, 3 with involutional melancholia, 2 with drug dependence, and 2 with adjustment reactions of adolescence. Only item 6 yielded statistical significance. The authors inferred:

> *The patients who think that the most important aspect of religion is that it offers the possibility of a life after death apparently have higher death anxiety. One explanation for this finding is that mentally disturbed people with high death anxiety tend to have a strong need for a religion-based belief in a life after death. An alternative explanation is that having religious beliefs that strongly focus upon an afterlife tends to produce high death anxiety in psychiatric patients.*

The *F*-ratio for item 4 just barely misses significance at the .05 level (see Table 2.3). Psychiatric patients who are not presently of the same religious affiliation in which they were brought up as children carry with them higher death anxiety. An explanation for this state of affairs is lacking at present; however, it is entirely possible that for psychologically disturbed people, a change from the religion of one's childhood brings about separation anxiety and a sense of alienation. Also, some religions threaten apostates with punishment after death; for example, Catholicism has traditionally taught that the torments of hell await those who leave and die outside the church.

PERSONALITY

MMPI and Other Anxiety Variables

The MMPI was administered to college undergraduates as part of the construct validation process of the DAS (see Table 2.5). The correlations are rather low, with the pattern of significance suggesting that the high-death-anxiety college student tends not to be seriously disturbed but to be an anxious, sensitive, introverted person likely to admit weaknesses and not likely to act out. However, it was felt that these generally low correlations could be a function of the limited psychopathology in typical college students. Therefore, the DAS and MMPI were completed by 32 psychiatric patients in a state hospital. Patient correlations tended to be much higher than those of college students, the highest correlations being .56 with schizophrenia, .49 with psychasthenia, and .47 with depression. These relationships were viewed as congruent with the clinical literature, which

TABLE 2.5 MMPI Correlation Coefficients

Scales	College students (N = 77)	Psychiatric patients (N = 32)	Inmates (N = 101)	Kidney dialysis patients (N = 40)	Wives of kidney dialysis patients (N = 40)	Huntington's chorea patients (N = 13)
MMPI						
L	.05	—.27	—.22*	—.19	.02	
F	.13	.41*	.09	.05	.43**	
K	—.43**	—.10	—.30**	—.44**	—.37*	
Hypochondriasis	—.04	.17	.17	.07	.27	.61*
Depression	.03	.47**	.25*	.21	.48**	.75**
Hysteria	—.01	.34	.13	—.15	.16	.40
Psychopathic deviate	—.24*	.35*	—.11	—.21	.13	
Masculinity-Femininity	—.14	.31	.17	.17	—.01	
Paranoia	—.09	.39*	.26**	.05	.22	
Psychasthenia	.04	.49**	.25*	.09	.18	.57*
Schizophrenia	—.08	.56**	.06	—.10	.11	.67**
Hypomania	.12	.16	—.19*	.09	.14	
Social introversion	.25*	.02	.26**	.28	.35*	
Welsh Anxiety Scale	.39*	.44*		.35*	.38*	
Welsh Anxiety Index	.18	.36*		.26	.45**	
Manifest Anxiety Scale	.36*	.48**		.30	.54**	

*$p < .05$.
**$p < .01$.

states that schizophrenics, obsessive-compulsives, and depressives are troubled by death-related matters.

Table 2.5 also contains the MMPI correlations for penitentiary inmates (Templer, Barthlow, Halcomb, Ruff, & Ayers, 1979), kidney patients receiving dialysis and their wives (Lucas, 1974), and Huntington's chorea patients (Gielen & Roche, 1979–1980). With the six sets of correlations, the regular scales of the MMPI that most consistently yielded significant relationships are *K* (in a negative direction), Depression, Psychasthenia, and Social Introversion, demonstrating that the high death-anxious person certainly does not appear to have a good sense of well being. It should be noted that the special MMPI scales of anxiety tend to yield larger positive correlations than the regular scales. Kuperman and Golden (1978) have provided additional information by confirming a positive association between DAS and the Manifest Anxiety Scale, as have Lonetto, Mercer, Fleming, Bunting, and Clare (1980) and Gilliland (1982) and Abdel-Khalek (personal communication, 1985). Scales of anxiety independent of the MMPI have also indicated a positive association with general anxiety; these include Spielberger et al.'s (1970) State Anxiety and Trait Anxiety (Lucas, 1974; Abdel-Khalek, personal communication, 1985; Ochs, 1979; Gilliland, 1982), the Levanthal Anxiety Scale (Smith, 1977), and the Anxiety Scale of the Hopkins Symptom Checklist (Loewen, 1984). Highly death-anxious persons are also seen as tense as measured by the 16PF (Neufeldt & Holmes, 1979) and score higher on the Neuroticism Scale of the Eysenck Personality Inventory (Templer, 1972a; Abdel-Khalek, personal communication, 1985).

Depression

Depression has been found to be positively associated with death anxiety (Templer, 1967, 1969, 1970; Ochs, 1979; Gilliland, 1982).* This relationship was also noted by Koocher, O'Malley, Foster, and Gogan (1976), using a death attitude measure of unspecified psychometric properties. In a study using the DAS with retired persons, it was reported that all eight of the subjects who had an MMPI Depression Scale score of 28 or above had a DAS score above the mean, prompting Templer (1971a,b) to say:

> *High death anxiety is part of a depressive syndrome in elderly persons. However, the prediction of depression on the basis of high death anxiety is possibly a less dependable inference than the inverse relationship. It appears reasonable that, at least in some cases, the high death anxiety of elderly persons may be primarily a*

*See pp. 26–29 for a discussion of Gilliland's findings.

concomitant of depression. In such instances, the high death anxiety may be alleviated when the depression is treated symptomatically by such proven modalities as electro-shock therapy and antidepressant drugs.

In a subsequent study, Templer, Ruff, and Simpson (1974) gave the DAS and the Zung Self-Rating Depression Scale at the time of admission and at discharge to 27 depressed patients from 20 to 56 years of age. These patients were treated with tricyclic antidepressant drugs. Although their death anxiety was not directly dealt with in any way, there was both a significant decrease in death anxiety and a significant decrease in depression. Furthermore, there was a significant correlation between the decrease in depression and the decrease in death anxiety.

Time Anxiety

Death anxiety is positively associated with apprehension about the passage of time. Giroux (1979) found the DAS total score to be positively associated with Calalresi and Cohen's Time Anxiety Scale; Vargo and Batsel (1981) reported an inverse relationship between DAS score and the Time Competence Scale of the Personal Orientation Inventory; and Bascue and Lawrence (1977) provided evidence to show the importance of perceptions of time to death anxiety. In this work, death anxiety was correlated with anxiety about time, while submissiveness was linked to the constraints of time, being possessive of time, and particular orientations toward time. And as can be seen in the work of Lonetto, Fleming, and Mercer (1979), the awareness of time is, in fact, a component of death anxiety itself. Of interest is that both Noyes (1980) and Greyson and Stevenson (1980) reported that the perceived expansion of time associated with near-death experiences influences anxiety about death, in most cases reducing it (see pp. 100–101).

Another intriguing relationship between time perceptions and death anxiety involves the life review process and reminiscing. It has been hypothesized that if the life review (no matter at what age it takes place) results in an acceptance of one's life along with a lack of guilt or concern about changing it, then an individual can face mortality with little fear. In contrast, despair, depression, dissatisfaction, fear of death, and a feeling that time is running out will result if a life review concludes that one's life has not been a success (Romaniuk, 1981; Butler, 1963; Erikson, 1959; Jung, 1934).

Unfortunately, these hypotheses will have to wait for the research literature to rid itself of inconsistencies and fill in the gaps with a sound theoretical framework. Yet the body of work on the life review does point out that wherever a perception of time permits "the time lived" to be seen as much greater than "the time left to live," death anxiety increases.

Existential Adjustment Variables

The evidence indicates that death anxiety is inversely related to psychological adjustment as defined by existential criteria. Wesch (1971), Pollak (1977), and Vargo and Batsel (1984) all found such a relationship between death anxiety and self-actualization as measured by the Personal Orientation Inventory (POI). An inverse relationship between death anxiety and Crumbaugh and Maholick's Purpose in Life Test has been reported by Brown (1975), O'Rourke (1976), Bolt (1978), and Sullivan (1977); Tate (1980) found death anxiety to be negatively related to the life satisfaction in elderly women; while Flint, Gayton, and Ozmon (1983) found life satisfaction to be positively associated with Dickstein's Death Acceptance Scale. Death anxiety has also been shown to be positively associated with the altered states of *vivia*, a word that describes the experience of being fully charged with energy and able to complete difficult tasks at ease. Death anxiety has been negatively associated with *death transcendence*, which is the state of accepting one's own death without regret, and with *mediative awareness*, which defines the experience of calm, detached, inner-centeredness (Morgan, 1976).

Schulz (1978) designed an ingenious study to test her hypothesis "that culturally derived and reinforced ways of affirming the self, such as the motive to achieve and the actual realization of success goals, act to shield the individual in American culture from death anxiety by repressing conscious death awareness." (Table 2.6 presents the correlations between death anxiety and need for achievement as a function of religious orientation.) Schulz's plausible explanation of her results is:

TABLE 2.6 Correlations* between nAch and DAS, Controlling for Self-Defined Religiousness

	Males (*N*)	Females (*N*)
Religious	.01 (68)	—.04 (101)
Nonreligious	—.33 (30)	.48† (17)
Not sure	—.76‡ (17)	—.39† (22)

*Pearson Product Moment Correlations.
†Significant at .05.
‡Significant at .001.

The cognitive mediator appears to be more crucial to the defense against death anxiety for the nonreligious (by self-definition) who seem more strongly attached to achievement orientation as a defense mechanism than the religious person. The "not sure" group of males shows an unexpectedly high inverse correlation between nAch and DAS, indicating a very strong attraction to the cognitive mediator as a defense, and the suspected need to embrace some form of self-affirmation in the face of indecision concerning one's world-view. This result appears to be consistent with the finding that death anxiety, in males at least, is directly related to cognitive disorganization (Schulz, 1977). The "not sure" group of females follows this same pattern, only with less intensity than the males. Nonreligious women, however, pose somewhat of a puzzle. The high direct correlation between nAch and DAS evident in this group points to high death anxiety accompanying high achievement motivation. In short, the success-achievement cognitive mediator does not work for them. The explanation may rest in sex-role complementarity. Achievement motivation is not highly regarded as a means of affirming the self for women in the traditional middle-class American community, which by and large, still adheres to the pattern of male as breadwinner, female as homemaker. Where the nonreligious male may embrace the success-achievement orientation as a way of reducing death anxiety by becoming "productively immortal," the nonreligious female does not have this orientation as a culturally reinforced option, since it is not considered a part of her traditional sex-role. It appears that for these women the desire to achieve tends to heighten death anxiety rather than decrease it. Their attempts to act out success-oriented behaviours result in frustration because the community does not recognize these actions as positive or appropriate.

Locus of Control

Death anxiety is apparently weakly related to external locus of control, with some studies showing that higher death anxiety is associated with externality (Tolor & Reznikoff, 1967; Stewart, 1975; Sullivan, 1977; Burnett, 1982; Sadowski, Davis, & Loftus-Vergari, 1979–1980; Kuperman & Golden, 1978; Litman, 1979) while others have failed to show significant relationships (Incagoli, 1981; Nehrke, Belluci, & Gabriel, 1977–1978; O'Dowd, 1984–1985). Internal locus of control has been found to be associated with higher scores on the Collett-Lester Fear of Death Scale (Hunt, Lester, & Ashton, 1983) and Dickstein's Death Concern Scale (Kuperman & Golden, 1978).

Self-Concept, Adequacy, and Distress

Death-anxious persons have a negative self-image. As reported by Aronow, Rauchway, Peller, and Devito (1980–1981) and by Neimeyer and Chapman (1980–1981, using the DAS and the Collett-Lester FODS), death anxiety is positively associated with discrepancy between perceived self and ideal self. Both Alcorn (1976) and Davis, Martin, Wilee, and Voorhees (1978) wrote of the negative relationship between death anxiety and self-esteem, which was supported by the 16 PF findings that higher death-anxious persons are less self-assured (Neufeldt & Holmes, 1979), while scores on the Tennessee Self-Concept Scale have been shown to be inversely related to DAS score (Casciani, 1976). A positive relationship between DAS score and conflict score of the Rotter Incomplete Sentence Blank has been reported (O'Dowd, 1984–1985).

More highly death-anxious persons also tend to have lesser social adequacy; that is, Smith (1977) found an inverse relationship between death anxiety and an interpersonal adequacy factor of the California Psychological Inventory. To add to this outcome, as they did for the self-concept, Neufeldt and Holmes (1979) found that highly death-anxious persons are less socially precise as measured by the 16PF.

Death anxiety is associated with general anxiety, depression, negative self-attitude, discrepancy between self and ideal-self, low need for achievement, low self-actualization, low experienced energy, external locus of control, lesser purpose of life, lesser time competence, time anxiety, bodily concerns, lesser psychological endurance, being a sensitizer, neuroticism, lesser mental ability, lesser social facility, and lesser ego strength.

Vargo and Black (1984) provided additional confirmation of these associations in their study of 50 first-year medical students. The results of their work indicated that death anxiety (measured by the DAS) was negatively related to California Personality Indices of well being (—.52), good impression (—.43), and self-control (—.30). Vargo and Black felt that these results suggested that "the stringent requirement of a medical school may induce increased self-doubt, insecurity and anxiety in stress-sensitive students." Loewen (1984) helped this suggestion along by reporting a positive correlation between death anxiety and the Interpersonal Sensitivity Scale of the Hopkins Symptoms Checklist. Of course, these results may also reflect on the medical school selection process as well. However, long-term studies are needed to examine the nature of the dynamic interchange between the person and his or her work, home environment, and anxiety about death.

Gilliland (1982) pointed out that of the correlations with psychopathology, the highest coefficients were with measures of subjective states, especially anxiety and depression. In view of this, he attempted to determine the relationship between the factors on the Death Anxiety Scale and a number of different psychometric indices of distress and to determine the location of death anxiety within the factor structure of a range of subjective state variables.

In this work, Gilliland used the DAS, Bendig's (1956) Pittsburgh Revision of Manifest Anxiety Scale, the State-Trait Inventory of Spielberger, Gorsuch, and Lushere (1970), the Beck Depression Inventory (Beck, 1967), the 10 subscales of Berndt, Petzel, and Berndt's (1980) Multiscore Depression Inventory, and the Mosher (1966) Forced Choice Guilt Inventory with 166 participants from a general population and 120 psychiatric patients.

Principal-components factor analysis of the DAS for the general sample yielded four factors with eigenvalues greater than 1.0. Factor 1 was labeled "Fear of Death and Dying" and accounted for 63 percent of the common variance. Items with the highest factor loadings were: "I am very much afraid to die," "I am not at all afraid to die," and "The thought of death never bothers me." Factor II, which accounted for 15 percent of the common variance, was called "Thoughts and Talk of Death," a label borrowed from Warren and Chopra (1978–1979), who assigned such to their Factor II. In this case, items with the highest factor loadings were: "The thought of death seldom enters my mind," "It doesn't make me nervous when people talk about death," "I am often distressed by the way time flies so very rapidly," and "The thought of death never bothers me." Factor III was labeled "Subjective Proximity to Death" and accounted for 11 percent of the variance; it was loaded on "I shudder when I hear people talking about a World War III," "I often think about how short life really is," "I am not particularly afraid of getting cancer," and "I am distressed by the way time flies so very rapidly." Factor IV, "Fear of the Unknown," accounting for 11 percent of the variance, contained items such as: "The subject of life after death troubles me greatly," "I am very much afraid to die," and "I am really scared of having a heart attack."

For the psychiatric patients, four factors emerged: Factor I, "Fear of Death and Dying," (for example, accounted for 50 percent of the variance). The items with the highest factor loadings were the same as indicated for the general population. Factor II, "Time," accounted for 21 percent of the total variance, loading on "I often think about how short life really is" and "I am often distressed by the way time flies so very rapidly." Factor III, "Horror of Death" (e.g., accounting for 18 percent of the variance) contained items relating to "The sight of a dead body is horrifying to me," "I fear dying a painful death," and "I shudder when I hear people talking about a World War III." Factor IV, "Obsession with Future" (accounting for 11 percent of the variance), was described by "I am not particularly afraid of getting cancer," "The thought of death seldom enters my mind," "I shudder when I think about a World War III," and "I feel that the future holds nothing for me to fear."

Tables 2.7 and 2.8 display the correlation coefficients of these DAS factors and DAS scale scores with other measures of subjective states for the general and psychiatric groups, respectively. The values in these tables show clearly that death anxiety is associated more closely with trait than with state anxiety. Also, the measures of anxiety tended to correlate more highly with death anxiety than do measures of depression. Probably the most interesting finding is that the general group Factor I was found to be largely unrelated to depression and general anxiety. Separate correlations with male and female

TABLE 2.7 DAS Correlations with Subjective State Variables for General Populations

		Factors			
Variables	DAS score	1	2	3	4
A-State	.26***	.08	.17*	.20**	.12
A-Trait	.47***	.02	.34***	.35***	.29***
Bendig Anxiety	.49***	.05	.36***	.34***	.34***
Beck Depression	.34***	—.04	.31***	.22**	.26***
Multiscore Depression Inventory					
Total score	.38***				
Social introversion	.03	—.02	.11	.04	—.06
Guilt	.38***	.07	.28***	.32***	.17*
Cognitive difficulty	.41***	.05	.26***	.37***	.22**
Pessimism	.40***	.04	.24***	.36***	.23***
Irritated	.16*	.15*	.09	.09	.04
Fatigued	.32***	.07	.34***	.26***	.02
Learned helplessness	.29***	.03	.22**	.21**	.15*
Sad mood	.27***	.11	.22**	.18**	.10
Low self-esteem	.21**	—.04	.15*	.13*	.21***
Instrumental helplessness	.19*	—.04	.06	.20**	.20**
Mosher Guilt Inventory					
Moral guilt	—.03	—.00	.03	—.04	.04
Hostile guilt	—.10	—.05	.00	—.10	.02
Sex guilt	.01	—.27***	.07	.07	.10

$^*p < .05$.
$^{**}p < .01$.
$^{***}p < .001$.

TABLE 2.8 DAS Correlations with Subjective State Variables for Psychiatric Populations

Variables	DAS score	Factors 1	2	3	4
A-State	.18*	.15	..06	.02	.17
A-Trait	.40***	.22**	.16*	.23**	.29***
Bendig Anxiety	.46***	.28***	.25**	.21*	.29***
Beck Depression	.36***	.22**	.18*	.08	.29***
Multiscore Depression Inventory					
Total score	.44***				
Social introversion	.30***	.09	.12	.16*	.28***
Guilt	.49***	.25	.26***	.24**	.31***
Cognitive difficulty	.43***	.20*	.22**	.31***	.25**
Pessimism	.42***	.16*	.14	.32***	.33***
Irritated	.13	.05	.05	.11	.06
Fatigued	.35***	.24**	.15*	.20*	.19*
Learned helplessness	.25**	.16*	—.01	.17*	.22**
Sad mood	.35***	.22**	.06	.24**	.27***
Low self-esteem	.42***	.15*	.22**	.27***	.30***
Instrumental helplessness	.22*	.02	.20*	.18*	.16*
Mosher Guilt Inventory					
Moral guilt	.16	.02	.14	.08	.17*
Hostile guilt	.04	.01	.02	.07	.03
Sex guilt	.01	—.19*	.24**	.0.5	.01

*$p < .05$.
**$p < .01$.
***$p < .001$.

subjects in the general group yielded similar findings. Factor I appears quite similar to the first factor reported by previous investigators (Lonetto, Fleming, & Mercer, 1979; Devins, 1979; Warren & Chopra, 1978–1979). Gilliland maintains that Factor I is a straightforward measure of death anxiety (e.g., "I am very much afraid to die"), in contrast to the other three factors that pertain more to obsessional thinking concerning death – its concomitants, ramifications, and implications. Apparently, it is these neurotically oriented factors of death anxiety that relate more highly to depression and general anxiety. Gilliland suggested that the first death anxiety factor could be viewed as fear of death and the other factors as death anxiety.

A secondary purpose of the Gilliland research was to determine the location of death anxiety within the factor structure of subjective state variables. Factor I was labeled "Anxiety," Factor II, "Depressive Mood," and Factor III, "guilt" (see Table 2.9). For psychiatric patients, Factor I was labeled "Depressive Mood State," Factor II, "Anxious Depression," Factor III, "Guilt," and Factor IV, "Death Anxiety" (see Table 2.10). It is noteworthy that with the psychiatric group but not with the general group, a death anxiety factor emerged. Gilliland went on to say that death anxiety becomes so much more dominating in the psychiatric patient as to warrant separate consideration.

PHYSICAL HEALTH

In general, there seems to be little relationship between DAS scores and somatic integrity. We have previously seen how the preponderance of studies show either little relationship between death anxiety and age or a very small

TABLE 2.9 Principal-Components Analysis of DAS for General Subjects

	Factors			
DAS item	1	2	3	4
1	.53	.21	.14	.42
2	.21	.79	−.05	.15
3	.26	.40	.25	.25
4	.03	−.03	.20	.17
5	.83	.04	.20	.11
6	.14	.00	.45	−.02
7	.53	.36	.20	−.05
8	.05	.38	.39	.26
9	.17	.34	.32	.11
10	.11	.13	.04	.75
11	.19	.16	.27	.41
12	−.04	.35	.48	.19
13	.14	.09	.50	.15
14	−.05	.25	.16	.34
15	.20	.16	.34	.12
Common variance accounted for	63%	15%	11%	11%

TABLE 2.10 Principal-Components Analysis of All Psychometric Variables for Psychiatric Patients

	Factors			
Variable	1	2	3	4
DAS	.24	.21	.04	.75
A-State	.50	.45	.02	.04
A-Trait	.37	.74	.10	.18
Bendig Anxiety	.40	.71	—.02	.27
Beck Depression	.34	.77	.06	.13
Social introversion	.54	.13	.16	.14
Guilt	.47	.49	.11	.36
Cognitive difficulty	.59	.49	.00	.28
Pessimism	.69	.34	.13	.20
Irritated	.21	.45	—.00	.03
Fatigued	.68	.30	.10	.16
Learned helplessness	.77	.34	.07	—.00
Sad mood	.88	.27	.05	.14
Low self-esteem	.71	.40	.10	.20
Instrumental helplessness	.49	.43	—.10	—.01
Moral guilt	.07	.07	.88	.14
Hostile guilt	.07	—.23	.76	.07
Sex guilt	.08	.18	.50	—.10
Common variance accounted for	72%	16%	7%	5%

negative relationship. Terminally ill cancer patients have demonstrated lower DAS scores than persons in the general population (Gibbs & Achterberg-Lawlis, 1978); patients receiving kidney dialysis, an average degree of death anxiety both in research by Lucas (1974) and Blakely (1975); and somewhat below-average death anxiety for patients with Huntington's chorea (Gielen & Roche, 1979–1980). Although an appreciable percentage of heroin addicts die from a variety of causes by age 40, the research of Katz (1981) indicated that the DAS scores of heroin addicts did not differ from those of nonaddicts. Furthermore, the DAS scores of high and low use heroin addicts did not differ. Hypertensive and nonhypertensive middle-aged adults were not found to differ in death anxiety (Sherwood, personal communication, 1984), nor were differences found for institutionalized and noninstitutionalized elderly (Myska & Pasework, 1978); but Tate (1980) did find a positive association between death anxiety and health problems in elderly women. And, Nehrke, Morganti, Willrich, & Hulicka (1979) found an inverse relationship between death anxiety and perceived health in elderly male VA domiciliary residents. However, Templer (1971a) found no significant relationship in elderly subjects between death anxiety and number of yes answers on the symptom and history checklist that comprises the somatic section of the Cornell Medical Index. And Neustadt (1982) did not find a significant relationship between death anxiety and perceived health with nursing home residents ranging in age from 66 to 99.

The scale of the relationship between death anxiety and physical health status points to the extensive use of denial. This denial is both adaptive and maladaptive. It is adaptive insofar as continual preoccupation with death is nonproductive and brings psychic death; it is maladaptive insofar as it causes avoidance of decision and actions germane to one's life and finality.

OCCUPATION

Death anxiety does not appear to vary greatly as a function of occupation. In an unusual study, Brown (1977) found that the average death anxiety scores of death-row inmates did not differ from those of correctional officers. Funeral directors, and others who work in funeral homes, did not differ from control subjects (Templer, Ruff, & Ayers, 1976); Johnson (1980) reported rehabilitation counselors to have death anxiety comparable to that found in the general population; and Ochs (1979) wrote that hot-line volunteers, cancer society volunteers, and PTA members have average death anxiety and do not differ from each other. Mulholland (1980, 1982) found that the death anxiety of nephrology social workers and social workers providing services in a non-death-and-dying population did not significantly differ. And within the nephrology social worker group, there was no relationship between DAS score and number of years worked with nephrology patients; while Pepitone-Arreola-Rockwell (1981) showed that psychologists, suicidologists, psychiatrists, and funeral directors did not significantly differ. In addition, Whittenberg (1980) found that medical, surgical, medical/surgical, and ICU nurses did not significantly differ, nor did death anxiety differ as a function of number of terminal patients cared for in previous months or whether or not a death had been witnessed.

Some differences as a function of occupation or field of study have been found. However, there is reason to believe that this association could be a function of both the death anxiety and the choice of occupation as meditated by certain personality factors. For example, Thorson (1977), using the Edwards Personal Preference Schedule, demonstrated that death anxiety is positively associated with succorance, majoring in social work, and being female; it is negatively associated with endurance, aggression, exhibitionism, being male, and majoring in business. Thorson states, "One might thus picture the person low in death anxiety as being more masculine, assertive and pragmatic, and the one high in death anxiety as being more feminine, passive and empathic." Consistent with Thorson's findings is the association of high death anxiety with the "A" end of the "A-B" psychotherapist-type continuum (Salter & Templer, 1979). The "A" psychotherapist is more effeminate, intuitive, empathic, emotional, and neurotic. Thus we see that the highly death-anxious person seems to be characterized by greater emotional sensitivity. Such a formulation could also be viewed as supportive of the finding that military officers have lower death anxiety than control subjects (Koob & Davis, 1977). Sivesind (personal communication, 1983) found education majors to have high death anxiety and related this finding to those of Thorson (1977) insofar as it would appear that teachers have a high need to nurture others.

Lattanner and Hayslip (1984–1985) divided their subjects into a death-related and non-death-related group. The death-related consisted of 20 funeral home personnel, predominantly morticians and embalmers, and 20 firemen/paramedics. The non-death-related group consisted of 40 persons from a variety of occupational settings such as restaurants, real estate offices, schools, universities, and churches. The two groups did not differ on total DAS scores or on the Fear of Death of Self or Fear of Dying of Self of the Collett-Lester Attitudes Toward Death Scale. However, the death-related subjects were significantly lower on the Collett-Lester Fear of Death of Others and Fear of Dying of Others Scale. The authors felt that these results called for an examination of death anxiety at a number of levels of awareness and of the role death anxiety plays in occupational decisions. Yet another study demonstrated that firefighters and policemen were generally higher on the Collett-Lester scales than college faculty and business students (Hunt, Lester, & Ashton, 1983).

Nevertheless, the possibility that occupation could in part determine the level of felt death anxiety should not be discounted. Denton and Wisenbaker (1977) found that nurses with a number of years of work experience had lower death anxiety than student nurses.

McCarthy (personal communication, 1985) found that ICU nurses had significantly higher death anxiety than ward nurses and that there was a negative correlation between death anxiety and the number of years of nursing. Whittenberg (1980) added to this relationship by reporting that nurses with five or more years of experience had lower death anxiety than those with less than five years. Ohyama, Furuta, and Hatayama (1978) found that Japanese nursing students had significantly higher death anxiety than other college students during their first two years but not in their last year of college. To further demonstrate this pattern of change in death anxiety shown by nurses, Telban (1980) did not find a significant relationship between anxiety and the number of deaths nurses encountered on their wards, while Kane and Hogan (1985–1986) did find that younger and less experienced physicians had more death anxiety than those who were older and more experienced.

Finally, Amenta (1984) reported that volunteers who worked a year or more in a hospice setting scored higher on purpose-in-life (Crumbaugh and Mahalick Purpose in Life Test), and lower on the DAS than men and women who left the program earlier. An interesting suggestion made by Amenta is that these assessments might be used to develop screening techniques for hospice workers and other volunteers. In addition, the point was raised that death anxiety may have had a meditating effect on the choice to become a volunteer (i.e., a person would select such work as a way of becoming desensitized to death anxiety). Yet Amenta felt that the day-to-day contact with the dying would probably raise anxiety to the level that such persons would have to leave.

DEATH OF SIGNIFICANT OTHERS

The relationship between death anxiety and experiencing the loss of significant others is not very clear. Cole (1978–1979) found that those persons who had lost a significant other within the past year had lower death anxiety; but Gibbs and Achterberg-Lawlis (1979) found lower death anxiety among terminal cancer patients to be associated with previous experience with a dying person with whom one had a close relationship. Litman (1979) presented evidence showing a rise in death anxiety throughout the course of the year following the loss of an immediate family member; Smith (1977) reported no relationship between death anxiety and loss of a loved one within the past year; and Slezak (1980) found that death anxiety was neither related to knowing someone who had died or to a personal near-death experience. The findings of Ochs (1979) seem to contradict both those of Cole (1978–1979) and of Gibbs and Achterberg-Lawlis (1978), as Ochs's subjects who reported the death of a close friend or relative within two years had higher death anxiety.

BEHAVIOR

The research findings suggest that a commonsense interpretation is appropriate, since death anxiety is generally found to be inversely related to participation in life-risking behavior. Kasper and Vesper (1976) found that college students who are motorcyclists have lower DAS scores than control college students, and the DAS scores of psychiatric patients who had attempted suicide correlated negatively with lethality of attempt and the risk level of the attempt and positively with the rescue potential of the attempt (Tarter, Templer, & Perley, 1974). Supportive of Tarter et al.'s findings is the research of Goldney (1981), which yielded a negative relationship between DAS score and lethality of suicide attempt. In terms of more general behavior, Templer (1972a) found that although the death anxiety of smokers and nonsmokers did not differ, there was a small but significant inverse relationship between DAS scores and number of cigarettes smoked per day. However, Berman (1973) could not replicate this significant inverse relationship.

More dramatic and violent forms of behavior were studied by Burnett (1982), who classified rape victims as "high resisters" if they fought back, screamed, ran, or tried to escape and "low resisters" if they did none of the above. They were instructed to fill out the DAS, the Dominance Scale of the 16PF, and the Brown Locus of Control Scale as they would have before the time of the assault. The DAS proved to be the personality instrument that most accurately classified those rape victims. The point-biserial correlation coefficient between degree of resistance and DAS score was −.55. The three variables of (1) death anxiety, (2) whether or not the rapist had a weapon, and (3) whether or not the victim knew the rapist yielded a multiple R of .82. Burnett emphasized that the rape situation is a high life risk, in the same category as a person being held up for money or a soldier being asked by the enemy to surrender. She states that a rape victim might be told that she should no more feel guilty for having surrendered her body than a soldier would for having surrendered his freedom to avoid death.

It would seem likely that there are death anxiety levels that are optimal for various life-risk situations. One would think for example, that having low-death-anxiety personnel would be advantageous for the military. In fact, Koob and Davis (1977) did find that military officers have lower death anxiety than controls. In an interesting and relevant study, Schulz and Aderman (1978–1979) showed that the terminal patients of physicians who had higher scores on the Sarnoff and Corwin Death Anxiety Scale lived longer than patients whose physicians had lower death anxiety. Apparently, physicians with greater death anxiety took more heroic actions to extend the lives of their patients.

Death anxiety can affect behavior in a variety of situations in addition to those that are life-risking. Many if not all of us avoid situations that would arouse death anxiety. Shady, Brodsky, and Stoley (1979) found that student nurses who did not volunteer for a second (behavioral) stage of their research project had significantly higher death anxiety than nurses who did volunteer. As noted on p. 33, Amenta (1984) found that hospice volunteers who left the program had higher death anxiety than those who persisted. Goldsmith's (1978) research indicated that an educator's comfort with respect to teaching a course or unit on death was inversely related to his death anxiety.

We recommend that research be conducted that explores the adaptive function of death anxiety. For example, more death-anxious cardiac patients could possibly exhibit greater compliance with their doctor's orders. It is even possible that the experimental increase in death anxiety in reckless drivers would improve their driving habits.

ADDITIONAL FINDINGS

Death anxiety has been found to relate negatively to a sense of well being (Aronow, Rauchway, Peller, & Devito, 1980–1981), ego strength (Templer, 1967), interpersonal trust (Dunagin, 1981), and number of friends elderly women have (Tate, 1980); it has been found to relate positively to dogmatism (Shepard, 1980), bodily concern (Elkins & Fee, 1980), and being a "sensitizer" (Templer, 1973; Handal, Peal, Napoli, & Austrin, 1984–1985; Kane & Hogan, 1985–1986), and to be unrelated to social interest (Winter, 1982).

The Dickstein Death Concern scale is also associated with being a "sensitizer" rather than a "repressor" (Tobacyk & Eckstein, 1980–1981); as has the Livingston and Zimet Death Anxiety Scale (Handal, Peal, Napoli, & Austrin, 1984–1985) and a measure made up of a combination of DAS and Collett-Lester FODS items.

Devins (1979) found an inverse relationship between death anxiety and attitude toward voluntary passive euthanasia in elderly patients but not in college students. Slezak (1980) did not find a significant relationship between death anxiety and any attitudes toward euthanasia in college students. Slezak ascribed the different results to the age difference of subjects and suggested that elderly persons may view euthanasia in a less abstract fashion. However, to complicate the picture, Minean and Brush (1980–1981) found in college students a positive relationship between death anxiety and belief in the right of people to commit suicide; Salter and Salter (1976) found that more death-anxious college students visited the elderly more frequently and were more willing to help them; and Hartshore (1979) found a negative relationship between death anxiety in college students and the amount of time they spent with their grandparents. Schulz (1977) found that highly death-anxious persons showed relatively more loss of self-concerns and that less death-anxious persons had relatively greater loss of other concerns; Kinlaw and Dixon (1980–1981) reported death anxiety to be positively correlated with fertility experiences, desires, and intentions with both males and females of less than high school education but not with men and women with at least a high school education. Neustadt's (1980) research demonstrated a negative relationship between DAS scores of elderly nursing home residents and their appraisal of the quality of the care they were receiving. Loewen (1984) found a positive relationship between DAS score and the Somatization Score of the Hopkins Symptom Checklist. The DAS correlated positively with the Neuroticism and Psychoticism Scales and negatively with the Extraversion Scale of the Eysenck Personality Questionnaire (Abdel-Khalek, personal communication, 1985). Finally, delta alcoholics (those who were unable to abstain for long but who did not tend to lose control, according to Jellinek) had significantly higher death anxiety than teetotalers who had significantly higher death anxiety than gamma (those who lose control) alcoholics (Kumar, Vaidya, & Dwivedi, 1982).

SUMMARY

What are some of the conditions that determine the level and correlates of death anxiety? It can be said that there are two general determinants of degree of death anxiety: one is general psychological health, the other is life experiences concerning the topic of death (Templer, 1976).

In regard to psychological health, the results of scores of studies almost invariably show death anxiety to be associated with pathology. Psychiatric patients *do* score higher than normal individuals. As will be described in Chapter 5, patients treated symptomatically for depression by tricyclic antidepressant drugs had a decrease in death anxiety, and that decrease correlated positively and significantly with decrease in depression.

In regard to life experiences, Templer, Ruff, and Franks (1971) found substantial correlations between the death anxiety of adolescents and their parents. The fact that the correlations were significantly higher for the parent-child dyads of the same sex and that the highest correlations reported were between the DAS scores of the two parents would argue for an environmental determination. Husband-wife death anxiety resemblance was also reported by Lucas (1974) and by Koob and Davis (1977). Sibling death anxiety resemblance was reported by Kirby and Templer (1976), and college student-grandmother death anxiety resemblance by Hartshore (1979).

Further evidence of the environmental impact upon death anxiety is provided by the decreases and in some instances increases in death anxiety that have come about where death anxiety interventions have been attempted (see Chapter 5). Both Boyar (1964) and McMordie (1982) found that death-fraught movies increased death anxiety; there is also limited evidence that death of another, a close personal encounter with death, and work experience as a nurse can alter death anxiety level.

Interesting confirmation of the interplay between death anxiety and life experience is provided by Mercer, Bunting, and Snook (1979), who focused upon possible differences as a function of the civil disturbances in Northern Ireland. With religion controlled for, death anxiety was found to be significantly higher in Northern Ireland than in the Republic of Ireland. The DAS item that differentiated the two localities to the greatest extent was "I fear dying a painful death," which can be seen as a function of the violence in Northern Ireland.

Although the evidence meshes well with a two-factor theory (e.g., psychological health and life experiences), it is not claimed that this conceptualization encompasses all relevant variables and phenomena. A third "factor," possibly of an existential sort, partially independent of both psychological health and learning (incorporating one's sense of how one fits into the scheme of the universe; how the life one leads conforms to this scheme; and how the fact of death renders life meaningless or meaningful), may be a necessary addition.

3

THE DIMENSIONS OF DEATH ANXIETY

Anxiety is the repression of death.

(Alan Watts, *Psychotherapy East and West*, 1973, p. 136)

In McMordie's (1978) review of approximately 24 scales that attempted to measure anxiety about death, one of the conclusions reached was that "the most often cited definition in the assessment literature has been Templer's (1970) description of an unpleasant emotional state precipitated by contemplation of one's own death." At about the time McMordie's review appeared, Schulz (1978) wrote that many of the inconsistencies in the death anxiety data will probably be clarified once researchers begin paying close attention to the *components of death anxiety* instead of treating it as a unitary concept.

An adherence to a unidimensional approach is quite easily seen in the large and still growing literature recording the search for the correlates of death anxiety, the Gilliland study being an exception, as seen in Chapter 2. Unfortunately, there have been far fewer studies exploring the underlying structures of death anxiety, as noted by Kastenbaum and Costa (1977). This situation is undergoing change, as reflected in the work of Pandey (1974–1975); Nelson (1978); Lonetto, Fleming, and Mercer (1979); Lonetto, Mercer, Fleming, Bunting, and Clare (1980); Durlak and Kass (1981–1982); Ramos (1982); Martin (1982–1983); and Gilliland and Templer (1983).

The multidimensionality of death attitudes was, at one point, thought to encompass temporal and spiritual orientations (Faunce & Fulton, 1958). This traditional view became more defined through the important works of Herman Feifel, in which death anxiety was seen to be made up of a surcease from pain and tribulation, reunion with one's family, loss of control, punishment, and loneliness. These aspects of death anxiety were influenced, according to Feifel, by developmental changes, religiosity, personal traits, socialization processes, and the perceived and/or actual level of threat. In addition, death anxiety could often combine contradictory attitudes, demonstrating its pervasiveness and complexity.

Extending Feifel's insights, Stern (1968) stated that in his clinical observations fear of death has its own place in an individual's development; he claims that it contains a projection of actually felt annihilation of self and ego, along with fears of being immobilized, suffocating, and vanishing into nothingness. These are sensations Stern ascribes to that which an infant experiences as a loss of mothering. The association drawn by Stern between death anxiety and early separation fears is and continues to be a strongly held contention that goes beyond the boundaries of the psychoanalytic school. Stern went on to report that in all patients who were defending themselves against the fear of death, there were feelings of depression, emptiness, and despair as well as "a phase of haziness" lasting for weeks at a time. These symptoms are remarkably similar to the experiences of the grieving and bereaved (Lindemann, 1944).

Lifton's (1973, 1979) views on death anxiety also contain an annihilation component as well as fears of stasis, and of separation; while Kavanaugh (1977) revealed that his four personal fears about death centered on the process of dying, his actual death, the idea of an afterlife, and the abysmal aura hovering around death.

A more psychometrically oriented approach was taken by Pandey (1974–1975) in his factor-analytic study of the death anxiety of different sex and racial groups. The results of this work and that of Pandey and Templer (1972) showed more communality than uniqueness across the subject groups with respect to concern with escape, depressive fear, concern about mortality, and sarcasm. Nelson and Nelson (1975) using oblique factor analysis, identified four dimensions of death attitudes: death avoidance, unwillingness to be near or touch the dead; death fear, a personal and general apprehensiveness about death (i.e., "I am very much afraid to die," "Everyone should fight against death as much as possible"); death denial, the inability to confront the reality and consequences of death on a societal and personal level; and a reluctance to interact with the dying.

ASSESSING THE STRUCTURE OF THE SCALES

In a 1975 study, Nelson attempted to produce a three-factor scale to overcome the criticisms of the lack of proper validity and reliability aimed at scales other than the DAS. A battery of 43 items was designed for this purpose; it was composed of three items from Nelson and Nelson (1975); two with "minor modifications" from the DAS; while the other items were "suggested" by the works of Sarnoff and Corwin (1959) and Dickstein (1972). Additional items were selected to represent a variety of death-related behaviors and orientations. Through the use of oblique factor analysis, three factors emerged that were labeled as follows: Factor I, death avoidance, loading on "I could lie down in a coffin without experiencing negative feelings," "Seeing a dead body would not bother me," and "I could sleep in a room with a dead body"; Factor II, disengagement from death, described by "If I knew an acquaintance of mine were dying, I would probably feel uncomfortable around that person," "I would rather not know if a member of my family had a fatal condition," and "It would be difficult for me to spend too much time with people who are dying"; and Factor III, death fear loading on "It does not bother me to think about my own death" and "I find it unpleasant to think about how short life really is." Since oblique factor analysis was used, these three factors are not independent of each other (i.e., r between Factors I and II = .44; r between I and III = .57; and r between II and III = .42). This is an important point, as the majority of factor-analytic studies depended upon either principal components or principal axis factor analyses which yield orthogonal (independent) factors.

Aside from the difficulties inherent in pooling items from different scales, Nelson did show the multiplicity of concerns underlying anxiety about death. However, the items developed in this regard have received little attention in the literature, which only adds to the problem of assessing the value of this battery in terms of its clinical or predictive usefulness.

Durlak and Kass (1981–1982) examined 15 death anxiety scales (completed by 350 college students) in order to clarify the multidimensionality of death anxiety. They seem to have fallen into the trap of using factor analytic techniques to "shotgun." This term is used to describe the ability of factor analysis to reduce and group information without benefit of a strong theoretical model. In this way, the emphasis shifts to "see what's there" rather than testing the outcomes against a particular theoretical position. What is disquieting about this study is (1) that only two other factor analytic studies were noted in the references (i.e., Nelson & Nelson, 1975; and Klug & Boss, 1976) and (2) that little mention is made of the psychometric problems involved in simultaneously examining scales with formats ranging from true-false to five-point Likert types.

What Durlak and Kass did show, in spite of the methodological issues raised here, is that the multiple aspects of death anxiety seem to account for the degree of overlap between the scales and their relative independence. This supports the findings reported in the Appendix on the intercorrelation between the various death anxiety measures, and it should, since the intercorrelations between the scales served as the input for the Durlak and Kass factor matrix. In particular, the DAS loaded on the same factors as the following: Factor I—Collett and Lester's Fear of Death of Self and Fear of Dying of Others, Dickstein's Negative Evaluation, Lester's Fear of Death, Nelson and Nelson's Fear of Death, Krieger et al.'s Threat Index; and Ray and Najman's Death Acceptance; Factor IV—Collett and Lester's Fear of Death of Others/Fear of Dying of Self, and Nelson and Nelson's Death Avoidance; and Factor V—Dickstein's Conscious Contemplation. In all these associations, the total DAS scale score was used, not its component scores, which had been reported in the literature prior to the publication of the Durlak and Kass study (i.e., Pandey, 1974–1975; Lonetto, Fleming, and Mercer, 1979; Scott, 1980).

The scales assessing death anxiety do appear to be tapping various components of such anxiety, but can we get a clear mapping of these components? The wisest course of action to take to accomplish this goal would be to examine the dimensionality of those scales, which have already proven their reliability and validity, in a variety of experiential (i.e., dealing with the dying, having been actually injured) and proxemic (i.e., having been in a life-threatening situation) settings.

NATURE OF DEATH ANXIETY: PROVIDING THE MAP

The Lonetto, Fleming, and Mercer (1979) study was designed to compare the factorial structures accounting for the responses to the DAS for Canadian students (N = 255), those in Northern Ireland (N = 315), graduate nursing students (N = 124), funeral service students (N = 79), and members of the Unitarian Fellowship (N = 83). These groups were selected on the basis of their degree of experience with dying and death, with the Canadian students having minimal experience and the Northern Ireland students and funeral service students having far greater experience. For example, Kastenbaum and Aisenberg (1972, 1977) have reported that about 92 percent of North American college students have not seen a dead body; while Mercer, Bunting, and Snook (1979) found that among Northern Ireland students, 48 percent of the Protestant females, 62 percent of the Catholic females, 55 percent of the Protestant males, and 89 percent of the Catholic males had had direct experiences with the civil disturbances in terms of being in or near an explosion or attack or having a close friend or relative killed or injured. The inclusion of the Unitarians provided additional contrasts to the funeral service students in view of the Unitarians' involvement in the Memorial Society. Nurses were chosen because of their role in caring for the dying.

Principal-components factor analysis with varimax rotational procedures was applied to the item responses on the DAS for each subject group separately. The number of factors extracted was determined by the scree test (Cattell, 1966). Factor scores were generated for each group and contrasted using multiple discriminant function analysis (Cooley & Lohnes, 1962) in order to focus upon the nature of differences between these groups.

Although unique group-specific factors did appear (i.e., concern over terminal illness shown by funeral service students and concern over physical changes by the graduate nursing students), these differences were greatly overshadowed by the communality of factors across all groups. In fact, linear discriminant functions failed to find distinguishing item patterns between the groups, and only 24.86 percent of the subjects could be correctly placed within their designated group (i.e., Canadian, Northern Ireland, funeral service or graduate nursing students, or Unitarians).

The death anxiety factors common to these five subject groups were classified as (I) cognitive-affective, (II) physical alterations, (III) awareness of time, and (IV) stressors and pain. These factors were arrived at through the use of Kaiser's (1967) method for relating factors from different subject groups. The cognitive-affective component (Factor I) of death anxiety shows concern about being afraid to die (items 1 and 5), appearing nervous when people discuss death (item 3), the frequency of thoughts about death and their effects (items 2 and 7), and being troubled by thoughts about life after death (item 10) and the future (item 15). Concerns over physical alterations (Factor II) include having an operation (item 4) and the viewing of a corpse (item 14). Awareness of time (Factor III) is clearly identified by items 8 and 12, which deal with the distress brought about by thinking how rapidly time passes and thoughts about how short life really is. The fourth common death anxiety factor (IV) is concerned with being afraid of dying a painful death (item 9), getting cancer (item 6), having a heart attack (item 11), and reacting to discussions about World War III (item 13).

These four factors are consistent with the views expressed by previous investigators (i.e., Kavanaugh, 1972; Lifton, 1973; Pandey, 1974–1975) and demonstrate that "the awareness of time" is independent of other aspects of death anxiety while accounting for 8.5 percent of the systematic variance of death anxiety responses across the five subject groups. This finding is supportive of the evidence presented in Chapter 2 (pp. 22–23), linking time perspective and orientation to anxiety about death.

It is also of some interest that concern over having an operation is joined by the horrors of viewing a corpse and not by disease or illness. Does this pairing of items reflect the feeling that we tend to see ourselves not as recovering from an operation but rather as dying from it? Another possibility is that we have joined these items under a subset of fears related to multilation, as pointed out by Natterson and Knudson (1960) and Bluebond-Langner (1978) in their work with fatally ill children; and to fears of hospitalization (see Kastenbaum & Aisenberg, 1972). To extend this line of discussion further, the fourth common death anxiety factor indicates that cancer and heart attacks are associated with fears of a painful dying process and not with hope about the future. The painfulness of dying was also found to be related to reactions to conversations about war.

What Lonetto, Fleming, and Mercer have achieved in their study is to set in place a framework for further understanding the components of death anxiety and give an illustration of the stability of that framework for groups with varying degrees of experience with death-related matters (i.e., in terms of the percentage of variance accounted for by the factor patterns across the groups). In a later study, Lonetto et al. (1980) showed the sensitivity of the component item approach over the use of total DAS scale score for describing the common and unique concerns of different subject groupings. In their study of Northern Ireland ($N = 315$, 88 males and 227 females) versus Canadian ($N = 255$, 109 males and 146 females) death anxiety responses, they found no significant differences in total DAS scores, as both were in the "normal" range (i.e., 7.02 for Northern Ireland subjects, SD = 2.90, and 7.18 for Canadians, SD = 3.27—with a mean age of 20.2 years, SD = 5.3, and 2.16 years, SD = 4.23, respectively). Nor did they find differences with respect to the relationships between DAS scores and Taylor Manifest Anxiety scale scores ($r = .34$ for Northern Ireland and .31 for Canadians). In fact, Templer (1969) reported the general range for such correlations to be in the mid-thirties.

Although total DAS scores did not show significant group differences, components of the DAS did successfully discriminate between these groups (Table 3.1). Subjects from Northern Ireland were more concerned about the shortness of life (loading on Factor III, "Awareness of Time") and the viewing of a corpse (loading on Factor II, "Physical Alteration"), which is understandable in view of the long-range effects of "the troubles" and the additional opportunities to view the dead that these have provided. In contrast, Canadians showed concerns about the cognitive-affective component of death anxiety (Factor I), which may be a reflection of their relative lack of experience with death.

On the item level, an intriguing difference between Northern Ireland and Canada was seen in the increased fear of getting cancer shown by the Irish students. A possible explanation for this difference can be made at two levels: (1) cancer is a symbol for "the troubles," as both are strongly associated with a painful death, disfigurement, and separation from the family; and (2) Northern Ireland students should show such concern, as the cancer mortality statistics for Northern Ireland versus Canada from 1960

TABLE 3.1 The Death Anxiety Factors Associated with Each of Five Subject Groups' Responses to the DAS (decimals omitted)

Factor	DAS item	Group responses	Loading*
		Canadian students (N = 255)	
I	4	I dread to think about having to have an operation.	—77
	1	I am very much afraid to die.	—64
	14	The sight of a dead body is horrifying to me.	—59
	3	It doesn't make me nervous when people talk about death.	—47
			(24.43%)†
II	12	I often think about how short life really is.	—85
	8	I am often distressed by the way time flies so very rapidly.	—71
	2	The thought of death seldom enters my mind.	—67
			(11.35%)
III	7	The thought of death never bothers me.	85
	5	I am not at all afraid to die.	—68
	15	I feel that the future holds nothing for me to fear.	49
			(9.04%)
IV	9	I fear dying a painful death.	72
	6	I am not particularly afraid of getting cancer.	70
	11	I am really scared of having a heart attack.	56
	14	The sight of a dead body is horrifying to me.	38
			(7.64%)
V	13	I shudder when I hear people talking about a World War III.	81
	15	I feel that the future holds nothing for me to fear.	45
	11	I am really scared of having a heart attack.	37
			(7.22%)

(*See footnotes on page 51.*)

TABLE 3.1 The Death Anxiety Factors Associated with Each of Five Subject Groups' Responses to the DAS (decimals omitted) (*Continued*)

Factor	DAS item	Group responses	Loading*
		Canadian students (N = 255) (*Continued*)	
VI	10	The subject of life after death troubles me greatly.	85
	3	It doesn't make me nervous when people talk about death.	55
	1	I am very much afraid to die.	48
	11	I am really scared of having a heart attack.	36
			(6.71%)
	Total σ^2 = 66.41%		
		Northern Ireland students (N = 315)	
I	5	I am not at all afraid to die.	82
	7	The thought of death never bothers me.	—60
	15	I feel that the future holds nothing for me to fear.	—59
	1	I am very much afraid to die.	—46
	10	The subject of life after death troubles me greatly.	—36
	3	It doesn't make me nervous when people talk about death.	—34
			(19.54%)
II	12	I often think about how short life really is.	—81
	8	I am often distressed by the way time flies so very rapidly.	—76
			(9.13%)
III	9	I fear dying a painful death.	74
	13	I shudder when I hear people talking about a World War III.	57
	6	I am not particularly afraid of getting cancer.	52
	7	The thought of death never bothers me.	47
			(9.13%)

(*See footnotes on page 51.*)

TABLE 3.1 The Death Anxiety Factors Associated with Each of Five Subject Groups' Responses to the DAS (decimals omitted) (*Continued*)

Factor	DAS item	Group responses	Loading*
		Northern Ireland students (N = 315) (*Continued*)	
IV	2	The thought of death seldom enters my mind.	76
	3	It doesn't make me nervous when people talk about death.	55
	1	I am very much afraid to die.	52
	11	I am really scared of having a heart attack.	52
			(7.77%)
V	4	I dread to think about having an operation.	66
	14	The sight of a dead body is horrifying to me.	65
	11	I am really scared of having a heart attack.	35
			(7.05%)
		Total σ^2 = 62.62%	
		Graduate nursing students (N = 124)	
I	15	I feel that the future holds nothing for me to fear.	84
	7	The thought of death never bothers me.	80
	5	I am not at all afraid to die.	77
	12	I often think about how short life really is.	63
	2	The thought of death seldom enters my mind.	58
	6	I am not particularly afraid of getting cancer.	43
	9	I fear dying a painful death.	30
			(27.51%)
II	1	I am very much afraid to die.	91
	10	The subject of life after death troubles me greatly.	83

(*See footnotes on page 51.*)

TABLE 3.1 The Death Anxiety Factors Associated with Each of Five Subject Groups' Responses to the DAS (decimals omitted) (*Continued*)

Factor	DAS item	Group responses	Loading*
		Graduate nursing students (N = 124) (*Continued*)	
	14	The sight of a dead body is horrifying to me.	60
	3	It doesn't make me nervous when people talk about death.	47
	6	I am not particularly afraid of getting cancer.	47
	8	I am often distressed by the way time flies so very rapidly.	47
			(18.49%)
III	4	I dread to think about having to have an operation.	—86
	3	It doesn't make me nervous when people talk about death.	—57
	13	I shudder when I hear people talking about a World War III.	—56
			(11.09%)
IV	11	I am really scared of having a heart attack.	78
	8	I am often distressed by the way time flies so very rapidly.	55
	2	The thought of death seldom enters my mind.	49
	12	I often think about how short life really is.	44
	3	It doesn't make me nervous when people talk about death.	—37
	14	The sight of a dead body is horrifying to me.	—34
			(7.62%)
V	9	I fear dying a painful death.	81
	13	I shudder when I hear people talking about a World War III.	55
	14	The sight of a dead body is horrifying to me.	—47

(*See footnotes on page 51.*)

TABLE 3.1 The Death Anxiety Factors Associated with Each of Five Subject Groups' Responses to the DAS (decimals omitted) (*Continued*)

Factor	DAS item	Group responses	Loading*
		Graduate nursing students (N = 124) (*Continued*)	
	8	I am often distressed by the way time flies so very rapidly.	—40
			(6.76%)
		Total σ^2 = 72.57%	
		Funeral service students (N = 79)	
I	11	I am really scared of having a heart attack.	84
	3	It doesn't make me nervous when people talk about death.	—31
			(22.90%)
II	13	I shudder when I hear people talking about a World War III.	—85
	6	I am not particularly afraid of getting cancer.	—80
	3	It doesn't make me nervous when people talk about death.	—50
	9	I fear dying a painful death.	—44
	4	I dread to think about having to have an operation.	—38
	15	I feel that the future holds nothing for me to fear.	—37
			(12.38%)
III	10	The subject of life after death troubles me greatly.	88
	1	I am very much afraid to die.	43
	4	I dread to think about having to have an operation.	33
			(10.98%)
IV	7	The thought of death never bothers me.	—90
	2	The thought of death seldom enters my mind.	—58

(*See footnotes on page 51.*)

TABLE 3.1 The Death Anxiety Factors Associated with Each of Five Subject Groups' Responses to the DAS (decimals omitted) (*Continued*)

Factor	DAS item	Group responses	Loading*
		Funeral service students (N = 79) (*Continued*)	
	15	I feel that the future holds nothing for me to fear.	—50
	1	I am very much afraid to die.	—41
	6	I am not particularly afraid of getting cancer.	—36
			(8.94%)
V	12	I often think about how short life really is.	—86
	15	I feel that the future holds nothing for me to fear.	—48
	1	I am very much afraid to die.	40
	9	I fear dying a painful death.	—34
	2	The thought of death seldom enters my mind.	—32
			(7.12%)
		Total σ^2 = 66.82%	
		Unitarian fellowship members (N = 83)	
I	14	The sight of a dead body is horrifying to me.	81
	3	It doesn't make me nervous when people talk about death.	80
	6	I am not particularly afraid of getting cancer.	54
	1	I am very much afraid to die.	40
			(22.61%)
II	10	The subject of life after death troubles me greatly.	—86
	9	I fear dying a painful death.	—66
	11	I am really scared of having a heart attack.	38

(*See footnotes on page 51.*)

TABLE 3.1 The Death Anxiety Factors Associated with Each of Five Subject Groups' Responses to the DAS (decimals omitted) (*Continued*)

Factor	DAS item	Group responses	Loading*
		Unitarian fellowship members (N = 83) (*Continued*)	
	1	I am very much afraid to die.	—37
	8	I am often distressed by the way time flies so very rapidly.	—36
			(13.22%)
III	2	The thought of death seldom enters my mind.	—86
	15	I feel that the future holds nothing for me to fear.	—62
	7	The thought of death never bothers me.	—45
			(10.67%)
IV	4	I dread to think about having to have an operation.	80
	15	I feel that the future holds nothing for me to fear.	49
	6	I am not particularly afraid of getting cancer.	—37
	1	I am very much afraid to die.	32
	13	I shudder when I hear people talking about a World War III.	32
			(8.94%)
V	12	I often think about how short life really is.	68
	11	I am really scared of having a heart attack.	66
	8	I am often distressed by the way time flies so very rapidly.	62
	7	The thought of death never bothers me.	47
			(6.38%)
		Total σ^2 = 61.82%	

*Only loadings ≥ .30 are included. Complete factor loading tables for each group are available from the principal investigators.

†Percent σ^2 accounted for.

through 1973 indicate that Northern Ireland rates, on the average, were 21.26 percent higher per 100,000 of population (as reported in the *United Nations Demographic Yearbook*, 1966–1974). For example, in 1960, 169.1 per 100,000 cancer mortalities were reported in Northern Ireland; the figure rose to 189.1 per 100,000 in 1973. Comparable figures for Canada showed 129.4 deaths per 100,000 due to cancer in 1960 and 149.5 in 1973.

It may be tentatively proposed that not only death anxiety factors but analyses at the item level as well should be considered in terms of making cross-cultural comparisons. To add to this notion, there was the finding that those items which discriminated between the groups had an average *r* value of .50 with total death anxiety scores for each group after their relative contributions to this total score were removed. Therefore, these items accounted for 25 percent of the systematic variance of overall death anxiety.

In terms of total DAS scores, a reasonable expectation would be that Northern Ireland students should have higher overall scores than Canadians. On the other hand, considering Frankl's (1955) work, it might have been expected that students from Northern Ireland would be less anxious about death than Canadians, as their sense of purpose in life may be heightened as a result of having to cope with the everyday experiences "the troubles" bring. In contrast, the life purpose of Canadians would be diminished as a result of a strong cultural emphasis on the acquisition of material goods as opposed to the growth of the individual. In spite of these speculations, the difference between total DAS scores for these student groups was not significant. In follow-up studies with the present and similar groups, detailed assessments of one's purpose in life should still be included in order to provide a better test of Frankl's proposition that people who have a high degree of purpose in life tend to be less anxious about death than those who feel that their lives lack such purpose.

Ramos's (1982) University of Madrid doctoral thesis "Personalidad, Depresion y Muerte" describes three separate principal components factor analyses (with varimax rotation) for 120 elderly, 110 students, and 244 hospital technicians. In each case, five factors were extracted, accounting for 55.5, 55.2, and 52.9 percent of the systematic variance of DAS responses, respectively. The major factor, again in each analysis, was concerned with the cognitive-affective component of death anxiety, contributing, on the average, 18.7 percent to the variance. The remaining factors were concerned with physical alterations, awareness of time, pain, and a combination of concerns that were difficult to label. Ramos concluded from these analyses that there are common death anxiety factors defying experience and age. To take this a step further, we might say that these factors can also encapsulate cultural differences.

The degree of one's actual experience with death has found its way into the work of Lonetto, Fleming, and Mercer (1979); Martin (1982–1983); Mercer, Bunting, and Snook (1979); and Ramos (1982), as noted above, but what of one's anticipated experience? Shepard (1980) asked counseling, nursing, and general education students to complete the DAS in terms of their personal attitudes and those they anticipate in the terminally ill. His results showed that the anticipated total DAS score was significantly higher for all three groups. These differences parallel those of Harris (1975), who found that younger persons show more fearful reactions to the perceived circumstances of the elderly than do the elderly themselves (i.e., concerning crime, health, finances, and so on).

From Shepard's factor analysis of the DAS, five factors were extracted for both personal and anticipated responses. The major factor under personal attitudes coincided with Lonetto, Fleming, and Mercer's (1979) Factor II—physical alterations; while a cognitive-affective factor similar to Factor I in the Lonetto, Fleming, and Mercer study was associated with anticipated DAS responses. Shepard's (1980) findings revealed that death anxiety is higher when there is increased concern about the cognitive and affective component of this anxiety, more so than when there is an increase in concern over physical alterations. In fact, the cognitive-affective component is the major factor associated with death anxiety in those factorial studies using varimax rotations. Therefore, fluctuations in its potency are directly transmitted to changes in the experience of overall death anxiety. These findings may also imply that in healthy persons, concern about this component is relatively low compared to thoughts about physical alterations, especially in those persons who have had little experience with the process of dying.

Keller, Sherry, and Piotrowski (1984), using a 12-item Death Questionnaire, reported a three-factor structure across persons ranging in age from 18 to 84 years. Middle-aged (38 to 44 years) and late-middle-aged persons (45 to 59 years) showed less anxiety about their general death evaluation (Factor 1) and self-related death concerns; (Factor 3) while the oldest persons (60 to 84 years) showed the least anxiety with respect to Factor 3. (Factor 2 was concerned with beliefs about the hereafter.)

The use of hospital personnel has also found its way into a number of death anxiety studies (see Chapters 2 and 5), including those described in this chapter; the work of Martin (1982–1983) continues along these same lines. The responses of 210 registered nurses from Canadian general hospitals to the DAS were factor-analyzed in the hope that their experience would manifest itself in the resultant factor patterns. The female nurses ranged in age from 21 to 59 years and brought with them from 7 months to 38 years of experience. Information was not included regarding the actual experience these nurses had with the dying and with death, although some of the nurses did work in intensive/coronary care units, surgery, and in the emergency wards.

Principal-axes analysis determined five factors which Martin called (I) death anxiety denial, (II) general death anxiety, (III) fearful anticipation of death, (IV) physical death fear, and (V) fear of catastrophic death. Upon examination of the items loading on Factors I and II, it appears that they represent a cognitive-affective component, while the items on Factor III load more heavily on the "awareness of time" (items 8 and 12) and less so on fears of pain, change, and the future. Factor IV involves fears of cancer and dying a painful death, which other investigators have labeled a stressor and pain factor. The last factor is really composed of one item, "I shudder when I hear people talking about World War III" (loading of .73). No attempt was made to relate these factors to years of experience or specialization.

Martin states that "the factor structure of the DAS with the present sample of nurses differed principally from those studies conducted with college students by the prominence of the 'death anxiety denial' factor." This difference is more apparent than real, owing to (1) the use of principal axes rather than principal components or oblique analyses, which have been used in the comparison studies, and (2) the subjective biases in labeling factors.

Gilliland (1982) and Gilliland and Templer (1985–1986) reported the response patterns for 166 subjects representing various civic and community groups (71 males and 95 females ranging in age from 18 to 73 with a mean of 31.1 and a standard deviation of 12.46 years), and 120 psychiatric inpatients (52 males and 68 females ranging in age from 18 to 69 with a mean of 35.5 and a standard deviation of 12.60 years).

Principal-components factor analysis with varimax rotation showed that civic and community members were most concerned about the cognitive-affective aspects of death anxiety (Factor I)—that is, "the thought of death never bothers me," "I am not at all afraid to die." Factor II combined thoughts and conversations about death and distress over the rapid passage of time. The theme of time being short was continued in Factor III, along with fears of cancer. Fears about life after death, dying, and having a heart attack were found in Factor IV.

Similar analyses of the responses of psychiatric inpatients produced an identical first factor to that of the general population, while Factor II joined awareness of time with the distress it can bring. The pain of dying and disfigurement in death were contained in Factor III; and Factor IV showed mixed concerns over World War III, cancer, and the future.

Gilliland and Templer felt that Factor I, which also appears in studies by Warren and Chopra (1978–1979), Devins (1979), and Lonetto, Fleming, and Mercer (1979), appears to be a more direct measure of death fears than the other factors. Factors II through IV are seen to be more indicative of obsessional thinking pertaining to death, of the ramifications of death-related behaviors and events. They propose that the first factor represents fears of death; the others, anxiety surrounding those fears.

It is not unusual for factors to shift around somewhat from study to study (see Table 3.2) since they are susceptible to the variances of different

TABLE 3.2 The Components of Death Anxiety

Fiefel
- Surcease from pain and tribulation
- Reunion with one's family
- Loss of control
- Punishment and loneliness

Lifton (1973, 1979)
- Fear of annihilation
- Fear of stasis
- Fear of separation

Pandey and Templer (1972)
- Concern with escape
- Depressive fear
- Concern about mortality
- Sarcasm

Ramos (1982)
- Cognitive-affective concerns about death
- Concern over physical change
- An awareness of the passage of time
- Concern about pain
- A mixture of concerns

Gilliland (1982), Gilliland and Templer (1985–1986)
- Cognitive-affective concerns about death
- Awareness of the passage of time
- Concern about pain and physical change
- Mixed concerns about physical change and time

Stern (1968)
- A projection of actually felt annihilation of the self and ego
- Fear of being immobilized
- Fear of being suffocated
- Fear of vanishing into nothingness

Kavanaugh (1977)
- Fear of the process of dying
- Fear of one's actual death
- Fear of ideas about the afterlife
- Fear of the abysmal aura around death

Nelson and Nelson (1975)
- Death avoidance
- Personal and general apprehensiveness about death
- Inability to confront the reality and consequences of death
- Reluctance to interact with the dying

Martin (1982–1983)
- Denial of death anxiety
- General death anxiety
- Tearful anticipation of death
- Physical fear of death
- Fear of catastrophic death

Lonetto and Templer (1981)
- Cognitive-affective concerns about death
- Concern about physical change
- An awareness of the passage of time
- Concern about pain and stress

subject groups and to the interpretations of various researchers. When taken as a whole, the factor analytic studies of death anxiety present a coherent, insightful, and sensible description of its structures—so much so that a number of studies have concluded that factor scores should be used in place of a global scale score (i.e., Martin, 1982–1993; Gilliland & Templer, 1985–1986; Nelson, 1978; Lonetto, Fleming, and Mercer, 1979).

FROM FACTOR ANALYSIS TOWARD AN UNDERSTANDING

The conclusions reached by the studies included in this chapter—whether arrived at by sophisticated psychometric methods, experience, or insightful speculation—tend to agree that there are about four factors that describe death anxiety. There also appears to be agreement on what to call them.

1. The major component or factor ties together both *cognitive and affective* reactions to death.
2. Another component focuses on the *physical changes*, real and/or anticipated, that accompany dying and serious illness.
3. An awareness of the unstoppable *flow of time* which can compress the future and expand the past is the third component.
4. The fourth component includes the *pain and stress*, actual and/or anticipated, brought about by chronic or terminal illness and personal fears.

These components not only provide clear-cut evidence for the multidimensional nature of death anxiety but also imply its universality. For death anxiety is a form, an often dramatic one, of anxiety about change and separation. Some additional evidence on this perspective can be found in the work of Richard Ulin (personal communication, 1985), who has been studying the death anxiety of Chinese adolescents. He has informed us that he has also found a structure encompassing intellectual and affective, physical change, true awareness, and pain and stress dimensions.

The structure of death anxiety can also provide a guide for tracing its intimate bonds with personal and cultural history. It may be used in this way because death anxiety has shielded, under its wide umbrella, two of the most powerful human conditions associated with our fears and anxieties—separation and change. In fact, much of what has been called death anxiety, if these components continue to hold their own in future studies, is produced by:

1. Concern about unknown reactions to the news of a death or serious illness

2. Perceived changes in our physical reality because of accidents, operations, war, or aging
3. Perceived alterations in the movement of time
4. Perceptions of how pain and stress can separate us from others and from the daily routine of our lives (i.e., as in grief and bereavement)

The components of death anxiety contain the experience of and reactions to change and separation. These experiences are fundamental to our existence, and so too is anxiety about death. We may have overlooked this aspect of death anxiety for too long; now we are facing the problem of how to see it for what it really is—an anxiety that enfolds many others, yet remains distinctive in its own right.

Feelings of death anxiety can arise when one or more of its components reaches a personally or socially defined critical level. But do we know which one component or combination will give rise to a sharply felt anxiety? Are feelings of death anxiety significantly different if they are founded on different component combinations, or are these feelings similar regardless of which components combine? And which combinations are necessary for personal and cultural survival? These and other questions about the impact of the components of death anxiety certainly need to be examined by both researchers and clinicians.

At the present time, there is a reasonably good concensus about what constitutes death anxiety. Now, we have to develop a perspective that allows us to look into and beyond these factorial pillars without losing our way. We have made a start in this direction by not relying so heavily on global scores of anxiety, which do reveal general trends but can hide far too much. Instead, our attention has been centering on the sensitivity of the components of death anxiety to personal (i.e., personifications of death) and environmental variables (i.e., a package left on a bench in a Northern Ireland railway station). Philosophical and theological perspectives have been examining these "pillars" for some time, and now psychology seems prepared to join them. It is our hope that by merging these perspectives, our understanding of death anxiety will open doors to our inner history as well as to an understanding of the relationships between survival and anxiety. This can then be translated into therapeutic strategies to help others cope with the effects and aftermath of death, change, and separation. We see this type of inquiry as an essential feature of the next wave of research. The first wave has supplied the necessary foundation blocks. Perhaps they are not as securely in place as some of us would like; nevertheless, they are there.

How the components of death anxiety develop and shift about in the adult years should be another feature of future research. The origins and development of death awareness in childhood is just beginning to make inroads into the developmental literature, almost 40 years after the work of

Maria Nagy and Sylvia Anthony. Less than 15 years ago, a popular misconception was that children under the age of 10 were not aware of death. A similar conception held today is that after the age of 12, our ideas about death remain largely unaltered (i.e., death becomes a logical/biological event that ends life). We need to challenge this conception in order to fully appreciate the complex nature of anxiety about death. We might find a good anchor point for this challenge in the so-called midlife crisis, which reflects a change in our awareness of time (i.e., the time we have left to live seems to be foreshortened, while the time we have lived expands and attracts us with a growing intensity).

Another question we will want along these same lines to ask is: Before children had an adultlike understanding of measured time, was the "time awareness component" a part of their anxiety? Or was there another one in its place, which gave way to concerns about time in the adult years?

Asking serious and meaningful questions is one thing, but trying to fit death anxiety, its components and correlates, into clean, neat little boxes is another. We strongly suggest that such "fitting" procedures be resisted. For example, to say that heroes feel little or no death anxiety while cowards are paralyzed by feelings that are too intense is to suggest a simple and direct relationship between behavior and death anxiety. To suggest that death anxiety has a $\cap$-shaped relationship be behavior, such that too little or too much results in maladaptive behavior while moderate levels can result in normal and adaptive behaviors is also too pat an explanation, although it does have some appeal.

Both of these examples at "fitting" death anxiety to an established model fail to consider that this form of anxiety is not like the others, as can be seen in its correlations with a number of traditional variables (i.e., sex, age, religion). This is the lure of death anxiety, along with the fact that a very small number of distinctive components have emerged from studies using a variety of methodologies. When such similar results are produced in this way, we must pay attention to them and try to understand them. And we are in the process of doing both.

4

DEATH IMAGERY

An individual psyche is determined by its beginnings and its end. An archetype of death exists and it joins all . . . in the same way birth does. Death defines life for us.

(McCully, *Rorschach Theory and Symbolism*, 1971, p. 154)

At the end of the previous chapter we began to add more humanistic concerns to our mixture of psychometrics and theory. In this chapter, this trend will be quite noticeable and necessary as we try to explore some relatively uncharted borders of death anxiety. This shift in orientation parallels a slowly developing trend, over the years, from concern about the physical processes of dying to the behaviors of the dying and health professionals' treatment of the dying, to an understanding of the role personal factors play in coping with severe illness and death. With this shift has come a renewed interest in the common and unique images of death.

A formless, dark entity may be the most well-known death image. Yet, this bleak void does not always signify fear. It has been associated with acceptance and/or reduced anxiety about death and an awareness of the balance between life and death as there is between light and darkness (Craddick, 1972; Lonetto, 1980, 1982).

The crossing of a river, in particular the Jordan and the Styx, has traditionally been a part of Western death imagery, representing a journey taken from the shores of the living to the land of the dead. Water symbols have carried with them a strange fascination, a timelessness, as they combine both death and resurrection seen, for example, in the act of baptism and the tides of the sea—with their ebb and flow becoming the rhythm of life itself, only to be ended as the tide turns:

. . . dying people never yielded up the ghost while the water was high. (Frazier, 1959, p. 69)

Sleep, the ace of spades, a black swan, a skull, the scythe and sickle, a black hand with a thumb pointing down, a broken column, an urn, a casket, a vulture, a flag at half mast have symbolized death in our culture (Lebner, 1956). Victorian cemetery art (Gillion, 1972) has provided further forms, such as a laurel wreath, a weeping willow, a golden bough or drooping flower, an empty bench, and an hourglass filled with the moving sands of time.

But of all the symbolic manifestations of death, none have provided so rich or historically important a channel for the expression of emotional and cognitive orientations toward life and death as *personifications* (Slater, 1963; Aries, 1974).

Craddick (1972) has suggested that the universality of death should be an indication that common or archetypical images must exist. At the same time, these images have a tendency to "change their shapes continually" (Jung, 1958). In view of the flexibility of death imagery, it seems like a good idea to explore these images, the fears associated with them, and their changes. First, we need to find a reasonable starting point. And, that is the period of middle childhood—a phase of development in which death personifications first appear with regularity.

THE MONSTER STRIKES: DEATH IMAGERY OF 6– THROUGH 8–YEAR–OLDS

It may be hard to believe that a person who stands about 46 inches tall, weighs about 48 pounds, and is missing a few teeth would think about death, but 6- through 8-year-olds do:

When I hear the word death, I think of some of the people that are dead that I know. And then I wonder how it feels to be dead. Not many people think about dying because everybody has to die sometime. So I just think about what I have to do day after day. (Susan, age 8)

Someone is dying because people are not getting along and if everyone keeps fighting, then people will not be friends. (Dana, age 8)

When I hear the word death, it makes me sad because some families have lost a person close to them. They will never see that person again. But the person who is dead is happy. (Catherine, age 7½)

During the "middle years of childhood" (as the years 6 through 8 are called), children experience their first major, and planned separation from home; they have to go to school! In addition to dealing with the problems of school—such as making friends, failing and succeeding, being criticized, and feeling different—many children are still working out their fears of thunder and lightning, of loud noises, of something hiding under the bed, and of the dark. This time in children's lives is also full of excitement and wonder as they explore the world outside of their homes.

Probably the most significant change in the way in which children understand the world around them takes place as they make the transition from home to school and back home again. Children now begin to see things in a different way than they did when they were younger. They begin to ask *why* things happen rather than *what* things are. As simple as this may seem, it has profound consequences that will forever change the child's relationships to events in his/her life. Children can come to the realization that there is a force outside their control that "makes things happen" even if they don't want it to happen. Adults may tell children that this force in the outside world is called "cause and effect." This is a powerful lesson for children, to learn that there is some force out there beyond them. They have to try to understand what this awesome presence is all about.

The child's awareness of death is affected by experiences at school, learning about cause and effect, and being away from home for longer and longer periods of time. Life and death are no longer seen as interchangeable as they were for 3- to 5-year-olds. Death becomes linked to those forces in the outside world and is described as:

> *. . . scary, frightening, disturbing, dangerous, unfeeling, unhearing, or silent. It takes you away but if you see death coming at you in time, you can escape. Death can be invisible like a ghost, or ugly like a monster, or it can be a skeleton. Death can be a person, a companion of the devil, a giver of illness, or even an angel. (Lonetto, 1980, p. 92)*

> *When I hear the word death I think of a skeleton and blood, ribs, skin. Somebody being killed with a gun, rope, or revolver and they should be charged with murder. (Paul, age 8)*

These death monsters may seem strange or frightening to adults, but they are the creations of the children (Figs. 4.1 and 4.2). The monsters have been drawn to help these children, other children, and adults to know what to look out for. It is important to be able to identify these monsters of death, so that you can escape from them. Children know there is enough time to escape if you see death coming for you. Unfortunately, this is not always the case for the aged and sick. Even if they could see the monsters in time, they wouldn't be able to get away and would be carried off to wherever the dead are taken.

Death, for 6- to 8-year-olds, comes from the outside world to carry off the old and the ill, but not children or their mothers. For 6-year-olds, about 22 of every 100 people get taken away by death monsters. Sixty-one out of 100 people meet the same fate for 7-year-olds, while 8-year-olds believe 75 out of 100 people die.

These 6- to 8-year-olds learn that old age and illness are *causes of death*, and that both come from the outside to attack adults. Children see "old age" quite differently from adults; in fact, being old for a child can be Tuesday of next week or being 15 or 29 years old. Other children feel that when people reach their 80s, the time has come for them to die.

FIGURE 4.1 Freddie (8 years, 4 months): "Death is a guy who had one eye and one no eye, one arm and half an arm. His hair is sticking up and he's frightening. He has a cut on his face. One half of his body is brown, one half is blue, he stands on little spikes." (Lonetto, 1980, p. 106)

FIGURE 4.2 Joey (8 years): "Death is a man with three heads. He is the person who makes you die. He is frightening and if you see him you get scared." (Lonetto, 1980, p. 107)

Interviewer: What happens when people die?
Angie (7 years, 5 months): They go into the ground, get buried, and then go to God.
I: Do they know they are in the ground?
A: No.
I: Why?
A: They are dead and they don't know anything any more.
I: What age would you like to die at?
A: 29.
I: Why?
A: Because it's sort of a good age but I may get into a car accident when I'm 29.

We actually know very little about children's ideas about aging; however, what we do know is that children are aware of the aging of their parents and grandparents. This awareness can lead to feelings of anxiety about the possible separation from, or death of, the child's parents. Sylvia Anthony (1940) presented the case of a small girl who wanted to place a large stone on her head so she wouldn't have to grow up, become old, and die like her parents.

Along with their interest in how to cope with death monsters and the aging of adults in their lives, children are very much concerned about the rituals of burial, what happens to the dead after they are buried, and how people die.

Death is when you are real old, you die or you kill yourself and the police may have to shoot a bad guy or your little brother or sister may drink poison and die. (Brian, age 8½)

Death means that you might get old and die and also get a heart attack and you might die. That means death. (Charlene, age 7½)

Interviewer: What is death?
Tod (8 years, 4 months): Death is when you grow old or somebody kills you.
I: What happens when you die?
T: You turn into sand.
I: Does the dead person know he turns to sand?
T: No.
I: How come he can't tell?
T: Because he can't feel.
I: Is there anything else a dead person can't do?
T: He can't breathe or talk.

The interest children take in burial rituals is a part of the uncertainty they have about the kinds of relationships the living and the dead are supposed to have. Children want to make very certain that the living and the dead are kept apart. Their curiosity about the rituals of burial marks a sharp break from their earlier ideas about life and death being reflections of each other (Lonetto, 1980). Now, death takes people away to be buried and then, hopefully, "on up to heaven and not down to hell." The living, on the other hand, are walking around on the earth in between the dead in the ground and those that made it to the sky.

As long as the living and the dead are to be separated, children begin to make the dead less and less like the living. The dead cannot move, eat, talk, hear, or easily return to join the living because they turn into dust or skeletons.

OLDER CHILDREN'S CONCEPTIONS OF DEATH

When children reach the conclusion that death is inevitable and universal (by the ages of 9 through 12 years), they have moved closer to the realm of adults (Fig. 4.3). Whether this is an achievement to be valued or not remains a question without an answer. Even if this question were examined, it is doubtful that a clearly articulated consensus would result. There would be agreement, however, that children's conceptions of death do change. The direction of change proceeds from death being a temporary state of living under different circumstances (for 3- to 5-year-olds), to death being a biological event ending life. Some older children have managed to avoid this biological interpretation in favor of seeing death in abstract terms as a vast blackness or a void (Lonetto, 1980, pp. 165–169).

But what is of importance is the order—children seem to have ended up with a view of death that is in opposition to the one they started out with!

FIGURE 4.3 Jelica (12 years, 3 months): "Brown to represent dirt; grey __________; black to represent darkness; red to represent blood." (Lonetto, 1980, p. 155)

This is a view that many children take into adolescence and their adult years.

Their new perspective of death as a biological event carries with it feelings of the fragility and mortality of the self. Young children did not allow any child to die, but with increasing age, death could penetrate the protective shell of children and those they love.

ADULT IMAGERY: PERSONIFICATIONS

Kastenbaum and Aisenberg (1972) reported that in North America death is most frequently seen as a male by both sexes. Perceptions of "death as a male" ranged from 61.0 percent for geriatric personnel to 90.6 percent for college students; perceptions of "death as a female" ranged from 3.1 percent for funeral directors to 39.0 percent for geriatric personnel (p. 163).

Greenberger (1965) wrote that an examination of death personifications could help lead to an improved awareness and regard of the dying person's perspective of death. The fantasies of critically ill female patients contained a number of sexual themes that were felt to be either a cause of anxiety or of comfort. Sexually arousing components of death fantasies have also been found for healthy females, but much less so for males (McClelland, 1963; Greenberger, 1965; Paris & Goodstein, 1966), while both McClelland and Greenberger have put forth the notion that women may look forward to death with some sense of excitement. Osis (1961) and Osis and Haroldson (1977) found themes of "death as a lover" in the accounts of hallucinatory episodes of terminally ill patients; and felt that "deathbed visions" serve to ease the transition to another plane of existence.

Although studies of sex differences related to attitudes about death have neither confirmed nor disproved the presence of systematically significant differences (e.g., Middleton, 1936; Diggory and Rothman, 1961; Christ, 1961; Swenson, 1961; Lowry, 1965; Lester, 1967a; Templer & Ruff, 1971; Lonetto, Fleming, Clare, & Gorman, 1976; Gilliland & Templer, 1983), there is a tendency for females to show more concerns about death than males. The greater fears displayed by females were specific to the death-of-the-self, the death-of-others, and the dying-of-the-self, but not to the dying-of-others or generalized fears of death (Kastenbaum & Aisenberg, 1977).

Of course, there are factors other than sex that contribute to death personifications, yet no clearly defined body of knowledge has appeared in the psychological literature pertaining to the nature of the influence of these factors. Sex differences seem so basic, but in spite of this they have revealed a remarkably wide range of associations with a number of variables related to death concerns (e.g., self-esteem, religiousness, health, etc.). Is sex so pervasive a factor that whatever the differences, they are rendered less meaningful, practically and theoretically? What seems to be missing is information about the relationship between person, the personification, and death anxiety.

In a study by Lonetto, Fleming, Clare, and Gorman (1976), the perceived sex of death for both males and females was correlated with death anxiety assessed by using the Handal Scale (1969) and the DAS.

One hundred and fifty students (67 males and 83 females), with a mean age of 29.8 years (age range from 20.0 to 49.0 years, standard deviation = 11.34 years), enrolled in psychology courses containing death and aging materials, participated. Linear discriminate function analysis was used to relate sex-of-student × perceived-sex-of-death combinations to item differences on the Handal and Templer scales. Linear discriminant functions are really special types of factors which summarize the most important differences between groups (Cooley & Lohnes, 1962). This type of analysis is used when groups of individuals can be defined a priori. In this study, students fitted into one of six possible groupings based upon their responses to the Death Personification Exercise (DPE: Kastenbaum & Aisenberg, 1977; Lonetto, Fleming, Gorman, & Best, 1975). The groupings were: males who perceived death (I) as a male, (II) as a female, (III) as sexless; and females who perceived death (IV) as a male, (V) as a female, (VI) as sexless.

The instructions for the DPE were: "If death were a person, what sort of a person would death be? Think of this question until an image of death-as-a-human-being forms in your mind. Then describe death physically, what would death look like? Now, what would death be like? What kind of a personality would death have?" Lonetto, Fleming, Gorman, and Best (1975) and Lonetto (1982) developed content coding categories for the DPE, one of which was the "sex of death" (see pages 71 to 72 for a detailed description of the coding categories).

Table 4.1 presents the correlations between four sex-of-student and perceived-sex-of-death groupings (functions)* and anxiety scale item discriminant scores. These correlations may be interpreted in much the same way as factor loadings.

Function I (males who saw death as male) shows concern with people talking about World War III, how short life really is, and the sight of a dead body as horrifying; no items from the Handal Scale were found as discriminators. Function II (males who saw death as sexless) is weighted with items from the Handal Scale related to seeing a dying person, feelings

*No male subject × Death as a female or female subject × Death as sexless groups were obtained.

TABLE 4.1 Correlations between Handal and Templer Item Discriminant Function Scores* and Sex-related Perceptions of Death Functions over All Five Sex-of-Student × Perceived Sex-of-Death Groups (decimals omitted)

	Items	I	II	III	IV
Handal Scale					
1	When I see a funeral procession, I never particularly wonder who the dead person is.	04	12	10	—16
2	My reaction to visiting the hospital where there are people who may have fatal diseases often includes certain disturbing and difficult to understand feelings of curiosity which are not altogether sympathetic.	—02	23	21	00
3	There are few, if any, real dangers to one's health while working on the wards of a hospital.	08	—15	*39*	*30*
4	We are kidding ourselves if we think cancer is not a hopeless disease.	—17	—08	—29	—10
5	Death hardly concerns me.	29	15	—13	27
6	People should cut out smoking.	03	04	—10	04
7	I hardly ever am troubled by such things as birthmarks or other marks on my body.	12	—01	18	09
8	Dying people don't make me uneasy.	07	—05	*48*	—02
9	At times one has the feeling that no disease is curable and one leaves the hospital in quite as good condition as they were before they fell ill.	—03	11	12	—08
10	After I am deceased I plan to donate my body to a medical school.	—06	05	06	—12
11	I wonder which of the diseases I know about will finally get me.	29	18	25	12
12	There is too much living to do for me to worry about death.	10	06	27	*32*
13	Sometimes you just don't want to see a dying person because he makes you feel pretty damned helpless.	—04	*51*	*30*	—01
14	Killing animals in a science course wouldn't bother me.	17	08	13	—07
15	A doctor has to be stronger than most to stand up to the constant emotional pressure due to suffering and death.	27	—02	12	—26

16	The thought of my dying young has hardly ever occurred to me.	05	—02	04	03
17	I think about death often; these thoughts accompany my life like the base accompaniment in music which I do not want to hear.	09	*—30*	01	*37*
18	Sometimes I've actually had some fantasies of the event of dying.	—05	08	07	—05
19	When I am ill it is certainly unusual for me to think of my dying.	09	—16	02	—19
20	I'd love to go into a field like medicine where maybe I could cure myself and live longer.	06	*—40*	—02	04
Templer Scale					
1	I am very much afraid to die.	—22	04	—06	—04
2	The thought of death seldom enters my mind.	15	05	00	*39*
3	It doesn't make me nervous when people talk about death.	29	04	11	*—32*
4	I dread to think about having to have an operation.	11	07	—25	04
5	I am not at all afraid to die.	22	14	*41*	*31*
6	I am not particularly afraid of getting cancer.	15	—16	02	—22
7	The thought of death never bothers me.	27	18	*37*	17
8	I am often distressed by the way time flies so very rapidly.	—25	10	—10	04
9	I fear dying a painful death.	—07	—12	—21	10
10	The subject of life after death troubles me greatly.	—21	21	11	—03
11	I am really scared of having a heart attack.	15	07	—15	15
12	I often think about how short life really is.	*—39*	—07	—06	15
13	I shudder when I hear people talking about a World War III.	*—43*	—05	—04	13
14	The sight of a dead body is horrifying to me.	*—35*	—05	—07	12
15	I feel that the future holds nothing for me to fear.	—07	*31*	11	07

*Correlations > .30 have been selected for discussion purposes and are in italic.

†Function I: Males who saw death as a male; Function II: Males who saw death as sexless; Function III: Females who saw death as male; Function IV: Females who saw death as female.

of helplessness, going into medicine to cure oneself and live longer, and thoughts about the future (DAS, item 15). The relationships of interest described by Function III (females who saw death as male) center around the dying person, the dangers of working in hospital wards, fears of cancer (Handal items 8, 3, 13, and 4), and cognitions about death (DAS, items 5 and 7). Function IV (females who saw death as female) reflects further cognitive concerns over death as they relate to conversations about death and personal thoughts about death.

In this study, females who saw death as female demonstrated the highest levels of anxiety. Comparable information on males who perceived death as female is, for the present, unavailable. Both males and females, healthy and ill, who personify death in terms of feminine characteristics are in need of extensive study before meaningful statements can be made about their respective approaches to death and to life. In contrast, males who could not identify the particular sex role of death consistently expressed less anxiety toward death.

Although the work of Lonetto, Fleming, Clare, and Gorman (1976), McClelland (1963), Greenberger (1965), and Osis and Haroldson (1977) has shown differences in male and female personifications of death while also suggesting differences in anxiety about death, we do not have enough information to build a theoretical model to account for the variety of differences reported. In fact, we do not know the order of effects or how their relationship can be moderated, and, more specifically, what dynamics are responsible for joining lowered anxiety with death seen as being nonsexual, as an abstraction.

The perceived sex of death is only one aspect of the personification process. What is the nature of the bond between a more complete picture of death and anxiety?

> *"Is death a personage, don Juan?" "What difference does it make?" Castaneda persists in this questioning. "Was your death like a person?" "Death is what everyone wishes. . . I am at ease with people, so death is a person for me. I am also given to mysteries, so death has hollow eyes for me. I can look through them, they are like two windows and yet they move, like eyes move." (C. Castaneda,* The Teachings of don Juan, *1972, pp. 190–191)*

Conceptions of life and death are inevitable, universal, and provide an essential bond between history and biology (Borkeneau, 1955; Lifton, 1976). However, studies have not systematically centered on the important features of the symbolic and cultural context in which death is perceived

(Bakshis, 1974), or on the complicated associations between death concerns and underlying psychological disturbances (Lester, 1967b). The work of Osis (1961), Searles (1961), Slater (1963), Lifton (1968), Greenberg and Blank (1970), Kastenbaum and Aisenberg (1972), Kastenbaum (1977), Templer (1976), Osis and Haroldson (1977), and Lonetto (1980, 1982) represent some contemporary exceptions.

Boulding (1965), Borkeneau (1955) and Jung (1933, 1958) have suggested that early death imagery remains throughout the life span and is firmly rooted in cultural and personal values and beliefs (as have Cassirer, 1953; Anthony, 1940; Nagy, 1948; Lonetto, 1980). As complete personifications of death are one of our most historical methods for coping with fear (see Lessing, 1769), it makes a good deal of sense to further explore the relationships between the components of these personifications and those of death anxiety.

Lonetto (1982) asked (1) undergraduates enrolled in courses in the psychology of aging, death, and dying ($N = 165$); (2) graduate nursing students ($N = 102$); and (3) funeral service students ($N = 68$) to complete the DAS and a Death Personification Exercise (DPE). These groups were selected for their interest and scope of experience in relation to aging and death (e.g., see Lonetto, Fleming, & Mercer, 1979). This sample had an overall DAS mean of 7.22 (SD = 3.24), with a range of 7.17 for funeral service students to 7.27 for graduate nurses.

The DPE used was a modification of the work of Kastenbaum and Aisenberg (1972, pp. 154–155). Instructions for the DPE have been presented previously in this chapter (p. 67). Twenty-five content coding categories were developed for scoring the DPE based upon the results reported by Kastenbaum and Aisenberg (1972); Lonetto, Fleming, Gorman, and Best (1975); and Lonetto, Fleming, Clare, and Gorman (1976) such that specific responses could be described by simple frequency counts. A score of zero indicated a descriptive category was not present, while a score of one or more indicated its presence. Multiples of one showed the presence of additional features; for example, the age of death perceived as aged (2), middle aged (3), youthful (4), a child (5), or timeless (6).

Coding Categories for the Death-Personification Exercise

1. Death as a *macabre figure*. A horrible, disfigured, ugly, and decaying, even to the point of skeleton-like, image of death.
2. Death as a *gay deceiver*. This image of death embodies many characteristics that are associated with the "good life." The gay deceiver seems to be both an ego ideal and a con man, poised, sophisticated, good-looking, and hedonistic.

3. Death as a *gentle comforter*. This image may be of an adult of any age but is usually portrayed as a wise and noble person.
4. Death as an *automaton*, a machine in human disguise, lacking in feeling and other human qualities, and totally objective in its point of view.
5. Death as a *void*, formless; dark, light, or multicolored; giving rise to feelings of coldness, warmth or wonder.
6. Other specific death images, such as a juggler, a mythological demon, an attractive dancer.
7. Coloring of death.
8. Bodily characteristics of death.
9. Sex of death.
10. Age of death.
11. Eyes of death—physical features.
12. Eyes of death—emotional features.
13. Face of death—physical features.
14. Face of death—emotional features.
15. Hair of death.
16. Hands of death.
17. Feet of death.
18. Walk of death.
19. Dress of death.
20. Speech of death.
21. Hearing of death.
22. What death is doing.
23. Reactions to what death is doing.
24. Positive emotionality of death.
25. Negative emotionality of death.

Intraclass correlations showed that rater reliabilities over all categories averaged .732.

Nine factors were extracted from the DPE content categories by principal-components factor analysis with varimax rotational procedures. The number of DPE factors was determined by the scree test (Cattell, 1966), while the DAS factors had been previously established for the present subject groups by Lonetto, Fleming, and Mercer (1979). In order to match DPE and DAS factors, factor scores were generated for each of the factors and then intercorrelated, following the procedures recommended by Nunnally (1967, pp. 367–368). Prior to the matching of factors, multiple discriminant function analysis was used to contrast DPE responses for each subject group.

Based upon DPE responses alone, only 17.24 percent of the sample could be correctly identified with respect to their membership group; that is, as university, graduate nursing, or funeral service students. Although funeral service students seemed to favor personifications of death as a "gentle comforter" while nursing students perceived death as a "gay deceiver," these tendencies were minor compared to the communality of personification themes across all three groups.

Over half (54.33 percent) of the systematic variance was accounted for by the nine DPE factors (Table 4.2). The first Factor (DPE I) described death as a "gay deceiver" and concern with the hands and feet of death. This attractive and beguiling figure is further humanized in DPE I by an awareness of the hands that reach out to touch and caress and the feet that are in contact with the earth.

DPE Factor II is more practical, as it deals with facing one's own death image in terms of *reactions to what death is doing* (i.e., feeling welcomed, hopeful, afraid) and what death *is* doing (i.e., welcoming, beckoning, reassuring, stalking). Along with these concerns is also an interest in the bodily characteristics of death (i.e., smooth-skinned, tanned, muscular, esthetic, hairy, large).

Death becomes a "gentle comforter" in DPE Factor III who has the patience to hear the living, and shows positive emotionality (i.e., kind, sympathetic, attentive, approachable). In DPE Factor IV, death is seen as "an automaton" dressed in human clothing. This is an emotionless, distant, and noncaring death whose eyes show no spark of humanity.

The "macabre" specter of death appears in DPE Factor V, and with it, concerns about the negative emotionality such an image can display (e.g., cruelty, impatience, violence, remoteness). The face, hands, and feet of the macabre death figure are further reflections of its negative emotional character (i.e., eyes that are cold and black, a face locked in a twisted or grotesque smile, large and powerful hands, and feet capable of great destruction).

DPE Factors I through V parallel the results reported by Kastenbaum and Aisenberg (1977), at the same time demonstrating the components of personifications of death are independent of one another. In addition, the four death personifications depicted in these five factors represent the predominant images in our culture that were first identified in the period of middle childhood (Anthony, 1940; Nagy, 1948; Lonetto, 1980). Of some interest is that the "gay deceiver" image (DPE Factor I, accounting for 11.04 percent of the variance) was extracted before that of the "gentle comforter" (DPE Factor III, accounting for 7.57 percent of the variance) and the "macabre" figure of death (DPE Factor V, accounting for 5.34 percent of the variance).

The remaining DPE factors continue the process of trying to find ways of humanizing, communicating with, and understanding the death that waits

TABLE 4.2 Principal-Components Factor Analysis of Death Personification Exercise Content Coding Categories (decimals omitted)

Category	I	II	III	IV	V	VI	VII	VIII	IX
1. Death as a macabre figure	00	—11	06	03	77	10	—02	13	—00
2. Death as a gay deceiver	71	07	—04	03	09	04	—07	—04	11
3. Death as a gentle comforter	—01	—15	—72	—02	06	16	16	10	08
4. Death as an automaton	04	—01	11	—77	—01	01	08	02	05
5. Death as a void	—09	—08	06	—00	—07	04	10	07	—74
6. Other images of death	—25	—15	30	30	—28	—26	19	—04	30
7. Coloring of death	29	15	02	—02	34	—28	—34	—16	—32
8. Bodily characteristics	02	—46	02	11	15	05	—25	19	39
9. Sex of death	—06	20	—04	—34	—04	17	—27	—45	14
10. Age of death	—22	—04	—19	—22	—24	36	—12	—20	—30
11. Eyes of death—physical	08	11	14	09	10	74	—13	—01	—05
12. Eyes of death—emotional	12	—22	—13	—33	24	42	08	—34	21
13. Face of death—physical	02	02	—20	—04	58	32	23	—23	04
14. Face of death—emotional	08	06	13	—12	14	—14	—12	—46	—02
15. Hair of death	—21	12	—08	—10	12	19	—53	—04	21
16. Hands of death	—43	11	—05	08	45	—10	—28	—27	06
17. Feet of death	—42	26	—01	—11	49	—08	—21	—06	08
18. Walk of death	00	—10	—08	13	06	06	03	—76	—02
19. Dress of death	—14	06	—00	—71	—06	—15	—11	03	—12
20. Speech of death	12	—14	01	04	—04	02	—77	—02	01
21. Hearing of death	—07	—04	—54	14	—02	—13	—10	—03	—14
22. What death is doing	—01	—68	26	02	13	—12	09	—22	—14
23. Reaction to what death is doing	—04	—72	—22	—01	—04	—01	—04	07	—03
24. Positive emotionality of death	19	14	—74	—02	—06	—10	—08	—21	17
25. Negative emotionality of death	16	—15	06	05	71	—04	—04	—11	09
Total % σ^2 = 54.33	11.04	7.57	6.88	5.56	5.34	4.82	4.69	4.44	3.99

to take us gently or by force, by persuasion or willingly. The physical and emotional qualities of the eyes of death and the age of death are associated with DPE Factor VI. Death was seen by 74.3 percent of males and females as being middle-aged or old. As shown earlier by Lonetto, Fleming, Clare, and Gorman (1976) and Kastenbaum and Aisenberg (1977), death is rarely if ever seen as a young person or obese and never as a child. In DPE Factor VII, the speech, hair, and coloring of death were joined together. It is as if all of this were in preparation for a rendevous with a stranger, and thoughts of the sounds of his voice, the way his hair looks, and how he will be dressed fill the waiting.

Descriptions of the walk of death (e.g., stealthy, light, airy, quick-paced) are joined with the emotional features of the face of death, and the sex of death in DPE Factor VIII; 82.3 percent of both males and females perceived death as a male, 10.6 percent saw death as female, and 7.1 percent could not assign death a sex role. Death assumes the qualities of a void in DPE Factor IX, and there is an attempt to shape this void into humanoid form, as seen in concern over the bodily features of death.

The four DAS factors, accounting for 65.76 percent of the systematic variance, have been described in Chapter 3 (pp. 56–57) as (1) cognitive-affective, (2) physical alterations, (3) awareness of time, and (4) stressors and pain. Intercorrelations between DPE and DAS factor scores tended to be in the low-moderate range (i.e., .20 to .30), revealing the following relationships.

1. Death as a "gay deceiver" (DPE Factor I) was related to the cognitive-affective component of death anxiety; specifically, to fear of dying, appearing nervous when people discuss death, the frequency of death-related thoughts, and being troubled by thoughts of life after death ($r = -.20$, $p < .001$).
2. DPE Factor II was associated with the physical alteration component of death anxiety (i.e., having an operation and the sight of a corpse; $r = .24$, $p < .001$); as was DPE Factor VII ($r = -.30$, $p < .001$).
3. The awareness of the passage of time (DAS Factor III; i.e., thinking about how rapidly time passes and of the shortness of life) was negatively related to perceptions of death as a gentle comforter (DPE Factor III; $r = -.26$, $p < .001$) and positively to death as being macabre (DPE Factor V; $r = .20$, $p < .001$).

These relationships demonstrate that imagination may serve to heighten or reduce aspects of anxiety. In particular, personifications of death as a *gentle comforter* and as a *gay deceiver* appear to be useful in terms of controlling or reducing anxiety about death, while *macabre* death imagery seems to be associated with increased levels of anxiety.

As reported earlier by Lonetto, Fleming, Clare, and Gorman (1976) and again in this study, lowered death anxiety was achieved by men and women who did not see death in sexual terms but rather as a spiritual light, a feeling, a great openness, or as a vivid pattern of colors.

At the present time, we can say that personifications of death illustrate interest in and fears of death; they are not in any way random displays. Personifications contain within their structures useful information about the nature of symbolization and of the meanings and purpose of life. We need to explore further the extent to which such imagery can be therapeutic and ultimately, curative.

> *Here is a story about three students, aged about 20, who went on a trip to the Alps for several days of mountain climbing. One day, they tried to cross a glacier and one of them fell into a deep crevice. One of the other two boys held the rope while he let his companion down into the crevice. When the rescuer reached the bottom, he saw his friend lying dead with his skull fractured. They could not pull up the dead boy so they crossed the crevice to the hut of the Swiss Alpine Club. While eating the dinner they had in their rucksacks, they saw a dwarf crawl out of the crevice and watched him cross the glacier and walk toward them.*
>
> *They panicked and ran into the bedroom, where they wrapped themselves in blankets and crawled under the beds to hide. As they had not come down from the mountain the following day, a rescue group came up and found them wrapped in blankets, still in severe shock and very frightened. They took the students to the hospital to treat them. Because the students could not tell of the fate that had befallen the third member, the doctors and parents felt that the boys had lost their sanity.*
>
> *Finally, the father of one of them told the story to his friend, the well-known therapist C. G. Jung, who replied, "Bring them to me and I will talk with them." They told Jung the strange and frightening story of the dwarf. Then he told them, "Well, you see, for thousands and thousands of years, our ancestors represented the dead as such tiny beings," and he showed them some icons, idols, little images of the dead flying around, and so on. Then he said, "All these things that our ancestors have drawn for thousands and*

*thousands of years are their way of representing forms of thinking (through and) about the world which is still within ourselves. In cases of emergency, accidents, and catastrophes, we fall back into representing what happens in these terms and that is what has happened to you.''**

*This story was told to Dr. Lonetto by Dr. Jacob Amstutz.

5

COPING WITH DEATH ANXIETY

> ***The existential school takes anxiety, Kierkegaard's angst, and its concomitant guilt as inseparable from being, since "to be" implies "not to be," and since to know fully that one exists will necessarily involve the dread of not existing.***
>
> (Alan Watts, *Psychotherapy East and West*, 1975, p. 132)

The major strategies described in this chapter are based on the contention that there are two basic determinants of the degree to which death anxiety is felt: (1) a person's overall state of psychological health and (2) his or her life experiences concerning the topic of death. If strong death anxiety is primarily a concomitant of a more pervasive psychopathological condition such as depression, an anxiety neurosis, obsessive-compulsive neurosis or schizophrenia, then the underlying syndrome should be treated symptomatically by psychotherapy, behavior therapy, drugs, or electroconvulsive therapy. However, if strong death anxiety is a relatively isolated symptom in a person who is otherwise psychologically healthy and if such death anxiety is a product of unfavorable environmental experiences, then death anxiety should be directly reduced by such behavior therapy techniques as desensitization. For many men and women, strong death anxiety is the product of more general psychopathology and specific death-related experiences. In this case, death anxiety should probably be treated by some combination of indirect and direct methods.

Although the studies included in this chapter deal with the matter of death, the reduction of death anxiety was not in all cases the primary goal. In some of the educational approaches, the sharing of knowledge was the ostensible objective; in the Zuehlke and Watkins (1975) study, an increase in purpose-in-life was the objective. Nevertheless, in all of the studies reported, a great deal of death-related material was presented in one or in a multiplicity of ways; in most, death anxiety was assessed before and after the presentation of these materials.

In outlining and reviewing these individual studies (concerned with death education and workshops, desensitization, and other coping strategies), the reader should pay special attention to the experiential versus didactic component, the intensity and extensiveness of the experience, the extent that active group processes were involved, whether there were follow-up measurements, and when they were taken (i.e., Kopel, O'Connel, Paris, Girardi, & Batsel, 1977; Oshman, 1978; Vargo & Batsel, 1984), and the resistance shown by death anxiety to being interfered with.

DEATH EDUCATION AND WORKSHOPS

Kirby and Templer (1975) determined the impact of a $2\frac{1}{2}$-hour death education seminar on the death anxiety of 17 social work students. The seminar consisted of three phases: (1) presentation of death-related material with group discussion; (2) exposure to a cadaver, followed by discussion of feelings about the experience; and (3) viewing a film of the final stages of a person's terminal illness and death. In addition, the students read Kübler-Ross's *On Death and Dying*. Six weeks following the seminar, these 17 students and 26 control social work students who had not participated in the seminar completed the DAS. The two groups did not differ significantly with respect to their anxiety scores, leading Kirby and Templer to conclude that the seminar had no appreciable and measurable impact upon their death anxiety. However, this study raised the often thorny issue of "when to make the criterion assessment," after one week, after two weeks, or a month or months later. This is a problem that plagues a host of studies, not only in the area of anxiety, attempting to measure change.

Murray's (1974) study is of importance because she was the first to include follow-up testing in her experimental design. Her subjects were 30 nurses who participated in an intensive six-week program of $1\frac{1}{2}$-hour sessions.

The first session introduced the topic along with the film *How I Could Not Be Among You*. This film dramatized in prose, poetry, and pictures the reactions of Ted Rosenthal, a young poet, over a period of time to the disease of leukemia and the knowledge of his shortened life span. The nurses were instructed to focus their attention on the poet's thoughts and feelings. What was he saying and how did he say it? What was he feeling and how did he show it? In the discussion that followed, these thoughts and feelings were discussed. Significant emotions relating to death were identified by the nurses in their interpretation of the music, prose, poetry, and interactions of colors and scenes, and brought out in the group discussions that followed the film.

Session two began with a presentation of the portrayal of death in art, music, and poetry from the time of the ancient Egyptians to the present. Printed material containing the words to selected musical compositions was distributed to facilitate sensory and emotional involvement with the music. The discussion centered on the nurses' reactions to the art work and musical compositions of a particular time in history and what it said to them about death.

Session three consisted of sensitivity awareness exercises. The participants were instructed "to use their memory and imagination to summon as many sensations, i.e., sights, touch, taste, smells, sounds of death as possible and to reflect on them." They were given crayons and instructed to draw their impressions of death. They were also told to write in a few words their feelings toward death. Discussion of the writings and drawings followed.

Session four centered around the defense mechanisms used in coping with death. There was a case presentation, followed by discussion on the mechanisms used by the patient, family, and staff to cope with death. Session five was intended to increase the nurses' experiential understanding of grief, while Session six attempted to assist the nurses through a personal experience of the reality of death. It was assumed that the basis of any program of death education was a personal, emotional approach to death. This was seen as necessary in that death education requires not only intellectual knowledge but awareness, on an intuitive level, of the phenomenon of dying. The choice of coordinator for this session was based on the assumption that someone who was having an intensely personal experience of dying would better act as a catalyst in assisting the nurses to face their own feelings about the reality of death. The coordinator for this session was a young man who had cancer. After a brief discussion of his own experience in facing death, he asked each nurse to write on a piece of paper how she felt about this. He suggested that each nurse ask herself who she would miss most when she died, what she wanted to accomplish before dying, when and how she wanted to die, who she wanted with her, and what she wanted done with her body after death. Discussion of this experience followed.

Murray reported no significant change in death anxiety scores prior to the program to the time of its completion. However, a significant decrease was found at the third administration four weeks later. Murray concluded that some sort of "consolidation" takes place during this time period, permitting death anxiety to "settle down."

Lockard (1982) designed a death intervention program for nurses which consisted of microlectures, audiovisual teaching, and discussion. The 37 nurses in the control group participated in seven two-hour sessions over a two-week period.

In the first session, the Kübler-Ross film *On Death and Dying* was shown in three parts, each of which was followed by discussion. The second session began with a 12-minute videocassette regarding the personal exploration of feelings about death and dying. This was followed by a group meeting in which the nurses were encouraged to talk about their own relevant feelings and anxieties. Session three began with a 17-minute videocassette regarding patterns of grief in different ethnic groups. In the discussion that followed, students were encouraged to examine ways in which death and dying was handled by their own families. Session four consisted of a microlecture and panel regarding communication with dying persons. Session five consisted of a microlecture on the death of loved ones, followed by discussion in which the participants shared personal experiences with the death of a friend or relative. A relevant videocassette presentation was assigned to each nurse after the class. Session six concerned the death of children. There were both microlectures and discussion that included personal feelings and anxieties about the death of a child. Session seven concerned care of dying patients and their families. This session included sharing personal feelings and anxieties about providing such care.

The 37 participants and the 37 control nurses completed the DAS before the program, immediately after, and four weeks following the completion. The DAS total scale score for the experimental subjects was significantly lower than before treatment, both immediately afterward and at the time of the follow-up, indicating a shorter "settling down period" than found for the group of nurses studied by Murray (1977).

Polderman (1976) developed three $1\frac{1}{4}$-hour sessions designed to reduce death anxiety in 82 college student volunteers. In the first session, there was discussion of three "symptoms" of contemporary American society ignoring the reality of death (i.e., the preoccupation with youth, the neglect of the elderly, and sham social customs such as using euphemisms like "passed away"). This was followed by further analysis of death-related experiences. Next, the subjects marked a point on a line representing 100 years to indicate the time of their death, specified their likely cause of death, and drew a picture to represent death. The final phase of session one consisted of reading two narrative personifications of death and the results of Russel Noyes's work "A Bliss Before Dying."

The second session began by pairing students and having them role-play a deathbed counseling situation followed by a group general discussion.

Then all pairs reversed roles, and this was again followed by discussion. The final exercise of session two consisted of a silent reflection upon what kind of lives the participants want to live, their deathbeds, and the extent that their actual lives approximated or differed from their idealized lives.

The third session consisted primarily of comparison of various philosophical views of death such as nihilism, the traditional Christian view, Jungian contention, existentialism. In addition, the participants were asked to think about what life without death would be like and to talk about their conclusions.

The 82 experimental subjects and 69 control subjects completed the DAS before the experimental strategy, immediately after, and six weeks later. Polderman stated that the effects of this form of death intervention strategy were not demonstrated.

The effects of death education on the death anxiety of high school students were studied by Bailis and Kennedy (1977) using 51 tenth-grade students enrolled in a six-week death education course which examined the sociological, psychological, metaphysical, and ethical aspects of death, with an interaction between activity and discussion. The activities consisted of field trips (to mortuaries, graveyards, medical schools), guest speakers (clergymen, morticians, doctors), and assigned readings (fiction, social sciences, and autobiography). These were followed by class discussions and written expression of the students' attitudes and concerns about death.

The DAS was administered to the experimental subjects during the first and last days of the course and to a control group not taking the course. As in the Kirby and Templer (1974) and Polderman (1977) studies, no marked effect on death anxiety was reported.

Edwards (1983) also attempted to determine the effects upon death anxiety of a three-week death education course for high school students. The 15-day course dealt with the topics of feelings regarding death, euphemism and words associated with death, loss, denial, Kübler-Ross's stages, funerals, grief, loss of self, and—on the last two days—the "celebration of life." The modes of learning included discussion, movies, lectures, an optional trip to a cemetary, the drawing of lifelines, an optional assignment to visit an elderly person, and bringing a symbol of life to the class.

The 30 participants in the course were 15 male and 15 female sophomores in a Catholic high school in Mankato, Minnesota. The 30 control subjects were 15 male and 15 female sophomores in another Catholic high school, also in Mankato.

The DAS was administered to both groups on the first day of the respective classes; three weeks later, upon the completion of the death education course of the experimental group; and a third time after an additional three-week interval.

Pre-post DAS differences were not significant for either group. The post to three weeks post-post difference did not approach significance for the control group, but there was a decrease in DAS score trend ($p = .11$) for the experimental group. This trend was found to be accounted for by a significant decrease ($p = .02$) for the females but not for the males. Although the reason for the sex differences in the Edwards study is not clear, it is here recommended that future research consider separately the effects of death intervention upon the two sexes.

Laube (1977) conducted a two-day death and dying workshop with 24 nurses, and described it in the following way:

> *The program was presented through lectures, films, and small group discussion and experiential work. At the beginning of the workshop, the focus was on the participant's death history and her feelings and attitudes about death and dying. The "pictures of death," included in this report, were drawn by the workshop participants as a non-verbal expression of those feelings. From there the program moved into the theory of grief, including the idea that one grieves any loss, whether it be a car, cat, patient, or a child. The workshop was concluded with principles and suggested interventions for working with the dying patient. At the end of the workshop, participants completed a course evaluation.*

The nurses took the DAS immediately before the workshop, immediately afterward, one month after the completion of the program, and three months after completion. DAS scores did not significantly change from pretesting to the completion of the workshop. However, scores were significantly lowered from the pretesting period to one month after completion. Yet this difference was no longer significant three months after completion ($t = 1.57, p < .20$), again, pointing out the difficulties in timing the assessment of change. Is there an optimum period for change to assert itself? An expected period of regression toward the original anxiety score?

The impact of a death and dying workshop employing *both* didactic and experiential group sessions was examined by Durlak (1979–1980). The participants were described as a cross-section of hospital personnel—physicians, nurses, ward medics, laboratory technicians, and the like. Each group participated in an eight-hour program which had two four-hour sessions on consecutive days.

The didactic presentations included lectures and discussions concerning helping patients emotionally to face death, personal feelings regarding death, emotional reactions involved in mourning and bereavement, social factors influencing the treatment of dying and grieving persons, psychological styles of adaptation to death, and the frequent denial of the reality of death.

In the experiential presentation, the participants performed Berman's (1972) Death Awareness Exercises, in which each person imagines he or she has only 24 hours to live and shares with the other group members how he or she would spend this last day. Durlak concurred with Berman that "this exercise produces strong affective reactions among participants and leads to intense personal discussions concerning anxieties, insecurities and fears about death and dying." The participants then became engaged in grief-related exercises in which the deaths of loved ones were discussed. Both the didactic and the experiential groups were shown videotaped interviews with dying patients and their spouses and given a didactic presentation of Kübler-Ross's work.

The DAS was administered from one to three days before and from one to three days after attending the workshop. The didactic group displayed a substantial and the experiential group a slight increase in mean DAS score. There was a highly significant time effect and a highly significant group × time interaction. Post hoc mean comparisons showed that the didactic group was significantly higher than the experiential but not the control group. The experiential and control groups did not differ from each other. Durlak suggested that the relatively favorable effects of the experiential method are brought about by the opportunity to "work through" death related feelings.

The effect of a death education program upon the death anxiety level of 91 persons—licensed practical nurses, registered nurses, nursing assistants, ministers, teachers, education directors, social workers, physical therapists, counselors, psychologists, speech pathologists, medical secretaries, housewives, and program administrators— was determined by McClam (1980b). They participated in a two-day workshop that included nine films, six group discussions, and three awareness exercises (e.g., "Draw your own personal picture of death").

The DAS was presented at the beginning of the first day of the program, at the conclusion, and four weeks later. There was no significant change either at the time of posttesting or at the time of follow-up. McClam (1980b) felt that the negative results were a function of the program not being sufficiently experiential. Is there systematic change in anxiety about death if an educational program contains experiential components, as the work of McClam and Durlak suggests?

Whelan and Warren (1980–1981) arranged a death awareness workshop intended to be experiential in nature to deal with the same phenomena that are represented in Kübler-Ross's five stages of acceptance of dying for terminal patients. The 16 participants were graduate students in counseling psychology and graduate education. Eight were randomly assigned to the treatment group and eight to the control group. The workshop was an eight-hour marathon. Reciprocal inhibition exercises were used to break down defenses associated with the stage of denial. "At this point, members were asked to imagine a situation which they perceived as a comfortable way to die. For example, an individual might imagine himself painlessly dying in his sleep. Members were led through the experience by directing their attention to each of their five senses and having them notice where they were, who else was there, what they were saying, and what their own feelings were. The imagery presumably stimulated the reality of each member's death and thus helped reduce the denial of death by increasing an awareness of its presence." Participants were revived from the state of relaxation and asked to share with the group their sensations. Group discussions served to further desensitize reactions to death as members heard the unique experiences of other participants. Strong experiential and group participation elements were also present in the other four stages.

No systematic effect of the workshop upon DAS scores was apparent four days after its completion, but it was reported that the workshop participants' mean DAS score was significantly lower after eight weeks. The authors inferred that cognitive reorientation toward death and emotional catharsis resulted directly from the workshop but that the lessening of anxieties about death occurred gradually. It seems then that change in anxiety can come about through specifically designed experiential exercises provided a reasonable period of time is allowed to pass in which assessments can be made. This still does not solve the problem of how much time is reasonable.

Thomas (1978) evaluated the impact of a weekend death laboratory on subjects who were volunteers from the North Texas State University and from the community. The 57 persons who volunteered were interviewed, and 18 of these were excluded because of one or more of the following conditions.

1. If acute depression existed during the interview as indicated by verbal self-report
2. If a significant death experience had occurred in the last six months
3. If acute anxiety reactions occurred due to discussion of death related topics
4. If the individual was unduly withdrawn or nonverbal
5. If the individual manifested an aversive interaction pattern or interpersonal style such as overly aggressive verbal behaviors or monopolistic verbal interactions
6. If the individual was currently receiving treatment for a diagnosed mental illness
7. If the individual obtained a score on the *Death Anxiety Scale* or *Self-Analysis Form* exceeding the 90th percentile on the initial screening

The remaining participants were assigned to either the experimental or the control group.

The activities included role-playing physicians telling patients they were terminally ill; marking X's on a "lifeline" to indicate their present point of time and when they will die; writing obituaries while imagining someone close had died; and group discussion of the above experiences.

Both experimental and control subjects were tested before and after the laboratory and in a follow-up four weeks later. Effects of the workshop were not demonstrated owing to the fact that *both* experimental and control groups showed decreases in death anxiety. Thomas also questioned whether Murray (1974) and Laube (1977) would have found significance had they used a control group, and the appropriateness of using as control subjects waiting-list volunteers.

Thomas (1978) noted that his high-death-anxiety subjects tended to decrease in death anxiety and his low-death-anxiety subjects tended to increase in death anxiety. He stated:

> *If this "regression toward the mean" effect is a valid observation, then using statistical treatment based on analysis of means would not produce significant findings. Furthermore, since the greatest degree of death anxiety reduction in the treatment group occurred for individuals scoring at the higher levels of death anxiety, it would seem that rejecting individuals on the basis of high death anxiety should be questioned.*

We have seen a confusing demonstration of the effects of death education and workshops on anxiety, ranging from no significant effect, to delayed effects, to an almost boomerang-like effect in the Laube (1977) study. What of the possible negative effects of such programs?

Wittmaier (1979–1980) evaluated the effects of a death course upon the death anxiety of 14 students in which most of the material was handled in a discussion format. The principal readings were Kübler-Ross's (1969) *Death and Dying* and Kastenbaum and Aisenberg's (1972) *The Psychology of Death*. Several ministers in a clinical pastoral care program met with the students, and a funeral director gave the students an intensive tour of his facilities. But, no pretesting of anxiety was carried out. However, both the 14 students enrolled in the course and the 20 control students who could not be accommodated into the course took the DAS two weeks after its termination. The mean DAS scores of the students who took the course tended to be higher ($p < .09$) than that of the control students. The authors stated, although not cautiously enough in view of the lack of pretest measures, that, "These results indicate that instructors need to be alert to the possibility that death and dying courses may have unintended effects." Such effects were not found by Nichol (1980) who investigated a four-week course on death taken by junior and senior high school students (102 students were enrolled; 103 were used as controls).

In contrast, McGee (1980) investigated the impact of an educational intervention death-and-dying workshop on death anxiety among middle-aged and older adults in North Carolina. The workshop consisted of six two-hour sessions spaced one week apart with relevant readings distributed at the end of each session. The author explicitly stated she intended the workshop to be experientially oriented.

The outline of the six sessions is as follows.

Session I: The Meaning of Life and Death

Aims: To help participants:

1. *understand some of the feelings and attitudes regarding death and dying prevalent in today's society;*
2. *examine their own feelings and attitudes toward death and dying;*
3. *understand that the meaning life has for an individual is related to the meaning death holds for that individual.*

Session II: Customs Surrounding Death

Aims: To help participants:

1. *recognize the universal human need for symbolic rituals in dealing with death;*
2. *understand some of the motives underlying cultural practices surrounding death in the United States;*
3. *understand that the customs and rituals surrounding death reveal an individual's or society's philosophy about death;*
4. *become more open in their willingness to discuss the topic of death through the sharing of feelings with other participants.*

Session III: Stages of Death and Dying and Alternative Care

Aims: To help participants:

1. *understand the various stages of the dying process and realize that these stages are experienced by most people;*
2. *become aware of various caregivers involved in the dying process;*
3. *reflect on how alternative care systems might help in the acceptance of death.*

Session IV: Handling Grief

Aims: To help participants:

1. *understand the meaning of grief;*
2. *understand the stages of grief;*
3. *examine their own feelings about grief;*
4. *become aware of roles that caregivers may assume with those in grief.*

Session V: Choices About Life and Death

Aims: To help participants:

1. *become more aware of many of the details involved in the dying process: estate planning, funeral arrangements and family affairs;*
2. *understand that through a fulfillment of life, death can become a fulfilling experience;*
3. *reach a closure between their past and present feelings about death and facilitate plans for the future.*

An example of a portion of the first session is:

A. Music Activity (15 minutes)

Music is very revealing. It reflects the pleasures, anxieties, concerns, problems, and doubts of people. Listen to the following songs about death and follow the words on the information sheet. While you are listening, think about these questions.

1. How is death pictured in these songs?
2. Do you agree with the images of death portrayed here? Why or why not?

As a total group, listen to the songs. Following the presentation of the songs, divide the total group into smaller groups of three per group. Restate the two questions and ask them to discuss the questions.

B. Discussion Activity (20 minutes)

After about ten minutes in the small groups, come together as a total group to discuss the questions. Spend a brief amount of time on question one, but spend a greater amount of time with the second question. The purpose of this portion of the session is to help the group members to verbalize and examine their own thoughts and feelings regarding death and dying. For many individuals, this may be the first time they have tried to put their thoughts into words for other persons. Some other questions which may help this discussion are:

1. *How do you view death? What is the meaning of death for you?*
2. *What do you think has most influenced your views about death?*
3. *Why do you think people fear death?*
4. *What do you fear most about death?*

You may not be able to deal with all of these questions because of time limitations. Use those which seem most appropriate within the time constraints you face.

Only seven items of the DAS were used. Items pertaining less directly to death and dying such as "I shudder when I hear people talking about a World War III" and "I often think about how short life really is" were dropped. The experimental group demonstrated a significant decrease in death anxiety from pre- to posttesting, but not the control group; while those persons having greater "fear of dying" as assessed by a questionnaire had a greater decrease in their modified DAS scores. This finding could be viewed as supportive of the observation of Thomas (1978) that persons with higher initial DAS scores exhibit greater reduction.

In addition, it seems that didactic approaches can increase defenses against death anxiety (Kopel, O'Connel, Paris, Girandi, & Batsel, 1977), while experiential approaches often lead to decreases in levels of fear of dying and personal death (Durlak, 1982; Vargo & Batsel, 1984).

> *Only by providing individuals with intense, personal experiences focused on immediate, death-related fears are educators likely to break through avoidance reactions and hence significantly alter . . . fears of dying and death. (Vargo & Batsel, 1984, p. 336)*

DESENSITIZATION

Since our readers may be from a wide array of disciplines, a brief description of desensitization seems to be in order. The *Dictionary of Behavioral Science* (Wolman, 1973) describes desensitization as simply "weakening of a response with repeated presentation of the stimulus" (page 96).

Although desensitization has probably been used for thousands of years, its widespread application by mental health professionals in the 20th century is often said to have begun in 1920 with the experimental work of Watson, the founder of behaviorism, and Rayner, his associate, with an 11-month-old boy called "Little Albert." Albert did not initially exhibit fear of a white rat but, after simultaneous presentations of a loud noise (the unconditional stimulus) with the rat (the conditioned stimulus), the rat without the loud noise was capable of eliciting anxiety. Watson and Raynor (1920) then proceeded to desensitize Albert by "constructive" activities such as feeding Albert in the presence of the rat.

Desensitization received its next impetus in the 1950s and 1960s from the work of psychiatrist Joseph Wolpe (1958), who employed the principle of *reciprocal inhibition*. It states that anxiety can be decreased by behaviors that are incompatible with anxiety, such as eating, assertive behavior, and relaxation. Wolpe utilized relaxation procedures in his *systematic desensitization* of phobias, in which the patient fantasizes feared objects or situations while relaxed or hypnotized. The phobic material is often arranged in a hierarchy of anxiety-eliciting potential, and the therapist and patient systematically proceed up the severity hierarchy when the patient feels relaxed.

Controlled research has also demonstrated that systematic desensitization is effective in the treatment of phobic conditions (Paul, 1966, 1967), while other research has indicated that a wide array of conditions respond favorably to desensitization, that the presentation of material in hierarchical order is not necessary in all cases, and that desensitization can be carried out in vivo as well as in fantasy.

Harlow (1976) compared the effects on death anxiety of nurses in group systematic desensitization, in vivo desensitization, and group systematic desensitization with in vivo desensitization. Only two nurses were placed in each of the three groups. The procedures Harlow followed were as follows.

> *(1) once subjects were relaxed, they were asked to imagine themselves playing the role of a nurse in a scene presented from the hierarchy, (2) subjects signaled (raising right index finger once) when they had a lucid mental picture of the scene, (3) subjects were to continue to imagine the scene until the author gave a verbal signal ("stop thinking about that"), (4) if anxiety was experienced while imagining a scene, subjects were to immediately signal him by raising and lowering their right index finger three times in succession, (5) if the scene was terminated as a result of either step 3 or 4, the subject was redirected to an awareness of her relaxed body state, (6) once a scene was terminated, the subjects were to give a verbal rating (0 to 100 point scale) of the amount of anxiety experienced during the previous scene, and (7) between hierarchy scene presentations, the subjects were occasionally asked to imagine a scene in which they would be very happy and calm.*

> *The group systematic desensitization procedure was standardized by (1) presenting all scenes at least three times to each systematic desensitization subject, (2) asking subjects to imagine each scene for three seconds for the first presentation, seven seconds for the second, and twenty seconds for the third, and (3) desensitization was thought to occur for a given scene when a nurse rated the scene 10 points or less after imagining it for at least twenty seconds.*

When each nurse had responded to all items of the hierarchy in accordance with the standardization procedures and rated all items 10 points or less, the treatment was considered complete.

The in vivo desensitization consisted of working with terminal patients. The systematic group desensitization with in vivo desensitization consisted of a combination of terminal patient care and the systematic group desensitization described above. Harlow was unable to determine the differential effects on death anxiety scores for the three treatment groups, and it is no wonder, with the small *N* used.

The use of in vivo systematic desensitization and systematic desensitization with symbolic modeling was incorporated into a study of 104 university students divided into two groups for four two-hour-per-week experimental sessions (Bohart & Bergland, 1979).

The first in vivo desensitization began with a muscular relaxation exercise, then each student constructed a lifeline depicting his or her life experiences. Following a period of dyadic and group sharing, each student was given an actual mortuary form to fill out. The session ended with group members relating to each other their feelings and thoughts brought out in the session. The other three sessions also began with the relaxation exercise. During session II, the groups were taken on a guided tour of a mortuary. In session III, they viewed a movie about a young cancer victim and were lead through a death fantasy trip in which they imagined their own deaths. In session IV, the group was visited by a person with a terminal illness. Then, the leader took the group through a death fantasy in which the individuals imagined the death of someone close to them. Finally, the group members completed, for this imagined person, the same mortuary form completed in session I.

The central issues for the systematic desensitization and the modeling group were the same as those for the in vivo systematic desensitization group. In session I, the in vivo members viewed a model on videotape completing the form and talking about her reactions to this exercise. In session II, a videotape of the model touring the mortuary was presented. In session III, the participants were given a manuscript synopsis of the movie rather than actually viewing it. They also saw the model on videotape participating in a death fantasy trip and describing her reactions to such. In session IV, a videotape of a model interviewing a terminal cancer patient was seen. Following this, another model completed a mortuary form for someone else and talked about her reactions to doing this.

Both treatment groups and the 36 persons in the delayed-treatment control group completed the DAS immediately before the start of treatment, immediately after, and three weeks after treatment. No significant differences were found in anxiety among the three groups at any of these points. Bohart and Bergland, in discussing their negative findings, stated:

> *The level and nature of death anxiety may be so well established that it may be impossible to effect change except through treatments covering extended periods of time. Admittedly, researchers frequently claim that their treatments would have been more effective if they only had had more time to deal with the threatening aspects and death anxiety that are so firmly entrenched. It seems clear that, given the years of learning that have gone into each person's attitudes regarding death, successful treatment may require more than four or five sessions. In any event, the nature of death anxiety cannot be disregarded in attempting to explain the results of this study.*

An example of a relatively successful indirect death anxiety intervention is provided by Peal, Handal, and Gilner (1981–1982) on the effects of group desensitization with university undergraduates. An important criterion for participation in the study was that the potential subjects be at least one standard deviation above the mean on the DAS scale. In addition to the desensitization group, there was a no-treatment (test-retest) control group and a relaxation group. Each threesome was yoked to the subject in the test-retest group to control for differences in treatment exposure due to working through the desensitization hierarchy at different rates. Both the desensitization and relaxation subjects took part in the relaxation technique of Goldfried and Davison (1976) for the first $2\frac{1}{2}$ sessions. The authors did not spell out the details of the desensitization but did state:

> *The desensitization groups also spent the first half of the third session learning to deepen their relaxation, but the second half of the session involved beginning to work through the death anxiety hierarchy in the prescribed method of desensitization. The desensitization groups continued to work through the hierarchy in the subsequent sessions.*

The process of "working through" was geared to the slowest person in each of the groups. When a desensitization group finished the hierarchy, each individual was retested immediately along with the individuals they had been yoked with in the other groups (relaxation and test-retest). The average number of sessions (approximately 35 minutes each) to complete the hierarchy was eight with a range of six to ten sessions.

The desensitization group mean fell from 9.00 to 6.23 ($p < .01$), while that of the relaxation group fell from 9.31 to 7.46 ($p < .05$). The test-retest group remained essentially unchanged. The authors appropriately inferred that the efficacy of the desensitization as a treatment of death anxiety was demonstrated. But they also wondered *why* relaxation training also lowered death anxiety, in view of the modest correlations between the DAS and measures of general anxiety. This is certainly a question that is in need of detailed and long-term study.

White, Gilner, Handal, and Napoli (1983–1984) were concerned about whether or not the positive effects of desensitization would last over time and whether this reduction would result in measurable changes in the behavior of health professionals as they interact with patients. Following the systematic desensitization procedures used by Peal, Handal, and Gilner (1981–1982), they evaluated the change in death anxiety on the DAS, Revised Livingston-Zimet DAS, and the Color Word Interference Test (CWIT) for nursing students at the St. Louis School of Nursing. These student nurses were placed in one of three treatments: (1) a desensitization group, (2) a relaxation-only group, and (3) a control group. Follow-ups were performed immediately after treatment and five months later.

The 23 nurses (22 females and 1 male) had reasonably high death anxiety scores to start out with (desensitization mean = 9.62, relaxation-only mean = 9.42, control mean = 9.00). Immediately after treatment these scores were 7.75, 6.14, and 9.12, respectively, indicating that both desensitization and relaxation only had positive effect on death anxiety, with relaxation only producing a more dramatic change. Five months later the desensitization group had an average death anxiety score of 7.71; the relaxation-only group mean was 7.00; while the control group mean rose to 10.00. These shifts in death anxiety confirm the results of Peal, Handal, and Gilner (1981–1982). But, they do more! They show that (1) relaxation only is a useful technique for reducing and stabilizing death anxiety, even more so than more elaborate desensitization procedures,* and

*Although the possibility exists that death-anxious persons may show what has been called relaxation-induced anxiety (Heide & Borkovec, 1983), increases in death anxiety have not been reported due to such training as they have been for general anxiety. Once again, we seem to be provided with evidence that death anxiety behaves differently than more generalized anxiety.

(2) that exposure to death-related material without benefit of relevant feedback may intensify earlier levels of anxiety about death. We need to explore the dynamics of elevated death anxiety scores in control groups and the possibility of clinical intervention.

This study further demonstrated the sensitivity of the DAS, over other measures of anxiety, to change, as the Livingston-Zimet DAS and the CWIT did not detect the up and down movements of death anxiety. Our concern about this study and others focusing on changes in death anxiety is that they continue to look at total scores and not at the components of anxiety. We still do not know which of the factors that define death anxiety have actually shifted! Certainly, at least one factor had to be affected by relaxation only—but which one? And, how?

Testa (1981) added a new dimension to group systematic desensitization programs by combining it with group implosive therapy to assess the death anxiety reduction of 48 female nurses. Thirteen nurses were assigned to group desensitization, 18 to group implosion, 19 to attention-placebo, and 11 to a no-treatment control group. The group desensitization and group implosion nurses had five 50-minute preprogrammed sessions in consecutive weeks. The nurses in the attention-placebo condition had five 50-minute weekly sessions in which they were shown films on death and dying. All the nurses completed the Likert format (McMordie, 1979) of the DAS, before, immediately after, and four weeks after the program.

The nurses in the group desensitization group were first exposed to systematic desensitization as developed by Wolpe (1958, 1973) and applied to a group setting (Lazarus, 1968). After training in muscle relaxation and visualization, a 27-item death anxiety stimulus hierarchy developed by Redick (1975) was introduced. The items ranged from relatively low on the apparent stimulus continuum (i.e., "I want you to imagine yourself being assigned to care for a 80-year-old man who has had several strokes and who is expected to die shortly" to "I want you to imagine yourself at the funeral of the person you love most just prior to and at the moment of death"). This group of nurses received six presentations of each hierarchy item, with the time of visualization increasing from 5 to 20 seconds. the nurses were instructed, when they felt anxiety, to raise their right index finger, stop imagining the hierarchy scene, and relax for 30 seconds.

For the implosive group, the principles of Stampfl and Lewis (1967), with the death scenario of Carrera (1977), were employed. The nurses were directed to imagine anxiety-arousing death scenes until such scenes no longer elicited anxiety—at which time they raised their right index finger. The scenario consisted of having a strange disease and being buried alive in a coffin. The scenario ended with the following vivid visualization experience of being trapped in a coffin.

And you rake your fingernails across the top of the coffin and you're scratching, you're scratching frantically like a trapped animal. You can feel the blood as it runs down your fingers and those torn fingernails, and you keep scratching and beating and turning. You can't turn over and your knees are hurting from beating against the top of that coffin and you're screaming, you're screaming, and nobody hears. And the air is getting thinner and you're panting, you are gasping, your blood is crying, your lungs are crying for oxygen. And it isn't there. It isn't there. All you are breathing is your own carbon dioxide. And you're feeling choked, and it's a horrible feeling. And now that there isn't much energy left in you but you're still making feeble attempts to claw the top of the coffin. And it's awfully hot. And it's a horrible sensation as you gasp and strain and hunger for air and it isn't there, it isn't there. You're choking and everything is starting to swim, everything is turning black. Everything is turning black. And you make one horrible last gasp for air and now everything is black. And you feel as though you're floating, you're floating through eternity. And you know where you're going, but you're floating, you're floating. Visualize that. Be there. Floating in the blackness of eternity. This is death. You're dead, you are dead. Experience it. You are dead. All right, this is the end of the fantasy. I'd like you to open your eyes.

As dramatic as this visualization exercise may appear, none of its effects even approached significance. Testa viewed his failure to obtain any death anxiety decrease partly to not having used subjects selected on the basis of high death anxiety. It will likely take many years of research and clinical work to provide a considerably more definitive picture of the role of desensitization in the treatment of death anxiety. At this time, we can say that desensitization will likely be more effective when high death anxiety is primarily a function of experiences pertaining to the matter of death than to matters of a more pervasive psychopathology.

If death anxiety displays a resistance to desensitization procedures, as it seems to for other than the highly death anxious, what of other interventions that may be better suited to deal with death anxiety as a state rather than as a trait?

OTHER STRATEGIES FOR COPING

Zuehlke and Watkins (1975) studied terminal cancer patients who were either given two weeks of Victor Frankl-based logotherapy or were assigned to a no-treatment control group. All the patients were asked to take both the

DAS and Crumbaugh and Maholvich's Purpose-in-Life Test before and after the therapy period.

> *The logotherapeutic steps undertaken in this study were as follows: Sessions 1 and 2 were designed to enhance development of rapport and to provide the therapist with information about various activities and people that had provided meaning in the patient's life. Later, this information was used to help the patient formulate new attitudes about his life situation. The second phase of therapy focused on the patient's feelings about hospitalization and his family's reactions to his current condition. The intent here was to guide the patient progressively in the direction of dealing with thoughts and feelings in the present. The third phase of treatment dealt with the fear of dying, unfinished business with relatives, and the patient's sense of self as no longer worthwhile. By use of Frankl's technique of dereflection, the patient was helped to shift his attention from the process of dying to areas of his life that he had earlier indicated provided meaning and satisfaction. The final phase of the therapeutic interaction involved an "interpersonal encounter," as described by Crumbaugh. This time was utilized to enhance a sense of closure for the patient and to provide him with the opportunity to relate as candidly as he desired with significant others, e.g., his immediate family, the therapist. This phase of therapy was usually a profound experience for the patient and served well the goal of developing more satisfactory coping abilities on his part.*

Logotherapy patients exhibited an anticipated and a significant increase in Purpose-in-Life score. However, there was also an increase in death anxiety. Zuehlke and Watkins's plausible explanation was that "Inspection of the change scores revealed that pretreatment scores for both groups were nearly one SD below the mean for normal death fears. After psychotherapy, the patients reported fears of death increased to an average level, which may indicate that the psychotherapy experience had the result that patients reported fears about their impending death that previously had been denied." The question to raise in this regard is what direction of change would have resulted if the patients had been highly anxious? Would there have been an appreciable drop in anxiety as other researchers have reported or would death anxiety have been pushed even higher?

It may make sense to suggest that high death anxiety is commonly part of a depressive syndrome in elderly persons. In such instances, death anxiety may be alleviated when the depression is treated symptomatically by such proven modalities as electroshock therapy and antidepressant drugs.

To test out this notion, Templer, Ruff, and Simpson (1974) assessed 31 depressed patients, 21 female and 10 male, in a state hospital. Nineteen were diagnosed depressive neurosis; 7 psychotic depressive reaction; 3 schizophrenia, schizoaffective type, depressed; and 2 manic-depressive illness, depressed type. They were given the Zung (1965) Self-Rating Depression Scale and the DAS within three days of their admission and these scales were readministered within three days of their discharge. Their hospitalizations ranged from 11 to 75 days with a mean of 28.87 days. Twenty-four patients received both tricyclic antidepressants (amytripyline or imipramine) and tranquilizers, usually of the phenothiazine type; two received only tricyclic antidepressants; and five received only tranquilizers. Most patients participated in group therapy, occupational therapy, industrial therapy, and recreational therapy. No attempt was made directly to remove death anxiety or to deal with it in any way.

The mean pretreatment and post-treatment Zung scores were 54.90 and 46.16, respectively ($t = 3.48$, $p < .01$); the mean pretreatment and posttreatment Death Anxiety Scale scores were 7.87 and 6.80, respectively ($t = 2.14$, $p < .05$); and the product-moment correlation coefficient between change in anxiety scale score and change in Zung score was .37 ($p < .05$). The authors stated:

The reduction in death anxiety which accompanied decrease in depression seems consistent with the contention that high death anxiety can sometimes be viewed as a symptom of depression. Since there was no control group given no treatment, it cannot be resolved whether death anxiety decreased as the depression spontaneously remitted or because the depression was reduced by treatment. Nevertheless, it appears that symptomatic treatment of depression and a decrease in death anxiety are related.

Antianxiety drugs, antipsychotic drugs, tricyclic antidepressants, and MAO inhibitors all seem worthy of evaluation. Perhaps behavioral techniques for the reduction of general anxiety or the treatment of depression will prove helpful as well.

In direct contrast to the external forms of management of anxiety provided by various drugs, more internally oriented techniques may also facilitate reductions in death anxiety; such as meditation. Curtis (1980) employed 12 subjects who had a minimum of three years of uninterrupted involvement in the practice of Zen meditation. She reported that they had significantly lower mean DAS scores than a group of 12 nonmeditators who were on the staff of a family service agency. This small sample aside, Curtis concluded that meditation may be helpful for reducing death anxiety. However, there was no assessment of death anxiety before meditation and, since comparability of the two groups is doubtful, this intriguing study should be regarded as providing hypotheses for further research on long-term coping mechanisms.

Although the changes in death anxiety found in the previous studies are not overpowering by any means, there are experiences that seem to bring about dramatic and sudden changes in anxiety. The uniquely disquieting, disruptive, and unexpected nature of *near-death experiences* does alter the course of death anxiety. We are discussing these experiences not to suggest in any way that they could or should be induced but to gain an understanding of the dynamics inherent in such experiences and how they influence the degree of death anxiety.

NEAR-DEATH EXPERIENCES

Picture yourself falling from a great height, your parachute has failed to open, and so has your reserve chute. You are falling . . . falling. The earth is coming up at you with ever-increasing size and ferocity. . . .

Your rope has broken and you are falling from a magnificent cliff. The side of the mountain is passing by you as you continue to fall and accelerate. . . .

What is going through your mind?

Greyson and Stevenson (1980) collected 78 reports of near-death experiences from three sources: letters to a national magazine from respondents who had read an article on near-death experiences, responses to announcements of interest in studying such cases in professional newsletters and magazines, and communications from people who knew of their long-standing interest in the nature of death experiences. What is surprising about all of this is that they collected only 78 cases! But for each of these cases a first-hand written report or tape-recorded account was collected, as was questionaire and interview material. In addition, Greyson and Stevenson examined medical records that were relevant to each of the near-death experiences.

At the time of their experiences, 27 percent of their samples were 18 years and younger, 32 percent were 18 to 35 years old, and 40 percent were 35 years or older. Sixty-three percent were women, 47 percent were married, 40 percent were single, and 12 percent were separated, widowed or divorced. All of Greyson and Stevenson's subjects were Caucasian. In 80 percent of their cases, medical personnel were present during or immediately after the experiences and 40 percent of the experiences were precipitated by medical illness, 37 percent by traumatic injury, 13 percent by surgical operation, 7 percent in childbirth, and 4 percent by the ingestion of drugs. In fact, in 47 percent of their reports, some type of drug or alcohol was taken on the day of the experience. What is also of interest here is that 67 percent of their sample reported that their near-death experience lasted for more than an hour.

What Is a Near-Death Experience?

An out-of-body experience, that is, the feeling of seeing oneself outside of one's physical body, was reported in 75 percent of the cases, and in 96 percent of these cases the actual leaving of the body was reported to be instantaneous and rather easy. As well, the reentry was reported as being effortless and instantaneous. About 50 percent of the 78 persons reported some sense of unity with nature, 37 percent the sense of God within themselves, 43 percent had the apparent memory of a previous life, 29 percent sensed auras, and 24 percent stated that they had communication with the dead.

In 31 percent of the cases, the reports included the description of passing through a tunnel, and in 57 percent of the cases, some sort of "point of no return" was reached in which the suggestion was that people somehow reach the edge or the interface between life and death. Perhaps one of the most significant findings of the near-death experience was the *displacement of time*, and in this study it was reported by 79 percent of the subjects. For example, 54 percent of this group reported that time seemed to pass more slowly than usual. This phenomenon of the slowing of time was associated with the appearance of unusual visual realities such as lights and auras, which were reported by 48 percent of the subjects. What is of interest here is that the awareness of the passage of time is related to a component of anxiety about death, and, in fact, accounts for about $8\frac{1}{2}$% of such anxiety. Why we say this is of interest in this situation is that individuals who reported distortions in their sense of time (i.e., the slowing of time) did not report high levels of anxiety about their death. In other words, the slowing of time seemed to act as a defensive barrier holding in check their anxiety about death, even though 52 percent of the subjects in the Greyson and Stevenson study reported that they believed they were actually dying during their near-death experience. What might also cause anxiety for people having a near-death experience is having their lives flash before them in some gigantic panorama in which every minute detail, every personal event of their lives, is shown on a giant screen. In fact, 27 percent of the Greyson and Stevenson sample reported such "panoramic memory" and in keeping with their sense of time displacement, such memories did not seem to occur in any given or logical sequence but rather all at once, in a simultaneous review of their lives.

The near-death experience was reported to be a very positive emotional experience by 15 percent of those going through it. Forty percent felt it was mildly positive, and 45 percent felt it either to be neutral or mildly negative. None of the subjects in this particular study reported their near-death experience to be very negative and the positive emotional effect of the experience was found to be strongly related to the degree to which subjective time is distorted. What this essentially means is that the more a person can slow down his or her own personal time, the more positive the near-death experience appears to be and, in particular, for those going through the experience who actually believed that they were going to die, the positive emotional repercussions were even greater.

We have to be careful in generalizing from the results of such studies, as this is a highly selective sample and certainly does not represent a cross-section of North American or even Western populations. But even in this small nonrandom group, we can see that the near-death experience can bring about a change or slowing down of personal time, which acts as a mechanism to reduce anxiety about the experience and induces a positive rather than negative feeling about the experience. What needs to be explored is the depth to which this experience affects one's daily life and the magnitude of the attitude changes in terms of later perceptions of time and of the self.

Noyes (1980) has extensively studied attitude change following near-death experiences and suggested that "some persons following cardiac arrest have claimed that being reborn has contributed a sense of uniqueness to their lives. Also, survivors of terminal cancer have reported dramatic changes in their attitude toward life, sometimes associated with spiritual enhancement" (p. 34).

Noyes examined the accounts of 215 persons who had survived life-threatening danger in a variety of ways: people's response to advertisements calling for accounts of subjective experiences during life-threatening danger, unsolicited reports of experiences in response to news items, and personal contacts. He interviewed 76 out of this sample of 215, using a semistructured interview. The life-threatening circumstances included falls (58), drownings (54), motor vehicle accidents (53), other accidents (24), and serious illnesses (26). A time period of three years had elapsed in 50 percent of the cases between the experience and the reports collected by Noyes from 144 men and 71 women.

Noyes reported a favorable attitude change resulting from such experiences, which is compatible with the findings of Greyson and Stevenson. In particular, such attitude changes included:

1. A reduced fear of death
2. A sense of relative invulnerability

3. A feeling of special importance or destiny
4. A belief in having received a special favor of God or fate
5. A strengthened belief in continued existence

Noyes also reported that these persons associated these changes with:

1. A sense of the preciousness of life
2. A feeling of urgency and reevaluation of priorities
3. A less cautious approach to life
4. A more passive attitude toward uncontrollable events

These results indicate that this particular combination of attitude change is part of good emotional health and well-being. But he cautions that not all people having near-death experiences come away with such positive feelings of health and well-being.

Forty-one percent claimed that their fear of death had been reduced following their accident or illness. From their reports, it seems that recognition of loss of personal control in the face of death seemed to bring a sense of peace and tranquility. For example, in a report in the *Toronto Star* on September 14, 1982, a parachutist performing in a show in London, Ontario, fell over 3,000 feet in front of 5,000 witnesses and survived. He is reported to have said that he decided there was nothing he could do about his situation and decided that since these were his last moments alive, he was going to enjoy them. He scanned the landscape and thought how beautiful it was to be falling through the air, and this would be his last view of the earth before his death. He also said that, as did the subjects in the Noyes, and Greyson and Stevenson studies, that this period of calm resignation seemed to be the most remarkable aspect of the experiences.

> *I never thought I would give up, but when I realized I could die, there was still no fear. Then I think the fear of dying left me. (p. 235)*

About 7 percent of the reports Noyes studied expressed the feeling that having survived a near-death experience, they were somehow no longer subject to death. That is, the wheel of fortune had picked them out on this particular day and it was quite unlikely it would happen again. Along with feelings of invulnerability, about 21 percent felt that destiny had spared them, that they were being saved for something in the future but they weren't quite sure what it was. What they were sure about was that God or fate or some other divine source of intervention had spared them because of their unique qualities or because of some unfulfilled task in life. In about 17 percent of the near-death experiences, God was seen as the responsible agent for this intervention. For others, nearness to death gave rise to feelings of urgency and a reassessment of their priorities in life, much like the awareness of the passage of time associated with the midlife dilemma. The nearness to death may also bring about a perception that each passing moment can be enjoyed for itself outside of a larger awareness of the passage of time; there is no urgency here, no moment beyond the moment that is being lived. However, this perception is threatened by a powerful and overriding sense of urgency about things that must be done, about the rapid unyielding passage of time.

A colleague of ours was making a telephone call and Dr. Lonetto was standing nearby, the operator put him on hold, he turned to Dr. Lonetto with a kind of mournful expression on his face and said, "Do you know what I'm feeling right now?" He was feeling that a few precious moments of his life were going by while he was holding onto the telephone. This black inaminate object was now the focus for his anxiety about the irretrievability of time, his time, and with each passing moment, there would be one less.

Not only does nearness of death bring with it an awareness of life, an urgency of the passage of time; but in some cases, a more open approach to living; and in others, a more passive approach was taken toward life as a result of this new death experience. In these latter cases (less than 10 percent), people simply stopped planning for the future because there was no way that any of their efforts could have the slightest effect on altering the future. These people saw themselves simply as pawns of fate; in defense, they simply gave up planning. In terms of the negative reactions to the near-death experience, from 3.5 to 12 percent of men and women reported a greater sense of vulnerability, helplessness, loss of control, and greater anxiety about death (i.e., for about 6 percent of these people, their near-death experience had brought on what might be called a phobic reaction to life itself in which cautiousness was the key factor determining much of their behaviors).

The reports of near-death experiences have a remarkable communality in terms of the relationship of the experience to the sensation of rebirth. As mentioned earlier, what seems to be happening here is that our earlier awareness of the fragile barrier between life and death is reasserted even for a brief time, and this brief reassertion signals a return to our earlier ways of thinking. What needs to be pointed out here is that the belief in rebirth is universal, at least in early childhood:

> *There was no anxiety, no trace of despair, no pain; but rather calm seriousness . . . and a dominant mental quickness . . . the relationships of events and their outcomes were overviewed with objective clarity. No confusion entered at all. Time became greatly expanded . . . a sudden review of the individual's entire past; and finally, the person falling often heard beautiful music and fell in a superbly blue heaven containing rosette cloudlets. (Heim,* Omega, *1972, pp. 45–52)*

The near-death experience allows us to become observers of ourselves and the events taking place around us, giving rise to a strange sense of the world, of the separateness and of the unity, of the meaningfulness and the meaninglessness. Many people going through this experience have difficulty in understanding how all this can happen simultaneously—how fleeting seconds are transformed into hours—and for some, how this strange time, seemingly between life and death, can lead to an overwhelming sense of unity, of inner calmness, and even lowered death anxiety.

SOME THOUGHTS ABOUT COPING STRATEGIES

On the basis of the studies included in this chapter, six general conclusions and some implications for future research can be drawn.

1. As Testa has pointed out, reduction in death anxiety is neither simple nor accomplished within a preset time frame. Very few studies demonstrated any change in anxiety, and even fewer a decrease (i.e., for those persons already high in death anxiety). It seems that death anxiety interventions may be limited by the fact that this form of anxiety is a fundamental and an inherent part of human experience and existence.

Death anxiety does have properties of a phobic sort as well as anxiety-obsessive properties. And, it can be aroused by certain stimuli more than by others, as is the case with a variety of phobias. Yet, death anxiety may represent an enduring, often engulfing or burdening condition that defies traditional psychological routes of escape.

2. In the majority of the studies that demonstrated a decrease in death anxiety, there was a strong experiential component. This is not to say that their programs did not contain a didactic element. However, in these studies, the emphasis tended to be on the vivid visualization of and intense concentration on death in its most undisguised and unmitigated form. Also, in these studies there was an increased bombardment of intense stimulus material and a deliberate affective and cognitive "working through" of this material. This "working through" was in the context of strong group

processes that included participation, empathy, and support (e.g., Durlak, 1978–1979; Laube, 1977; Lockard, 1982; Vargo & Batsel, 1984).

In the Peal, Handal, and Gilner (1981–1982) study, the desensitization and relaxation of the degree of death confrontation and the working through process could not be determined from their article. However, a distinctive feature of this study was that subjects were selected on the basis of having high death anxiety to begin with. Common sense dictates that there is more room for improvement with a higher degree of a pathological entity. An analogy might be that a greater tranquilization effect from a phenothiazine could be observed in a schizophrenic than in a neurotic. If subjects are unselected with respect to death anxiety, which was the case with the other studies, one may be dealing with some subjects with DAS scores between 2.0 and 3.0 at pretesting.

It should be noted that in all the relatively successful death anxiety intervention studies, the participants were also very involved both in regard to intensity and duration, in addition to displaying relatively high initial levels of anxiety.

3. About 50 percent of the studies reporting changes in death anxiety were not able to demonstrate a significant effect until follow-up testing several weeks after the program. Since only four of the unsuccessful studies (yielding no change or increased death anxiety) employed at least one follow-up measurement, some of these other "unsuccessful" studies might have shown different outcomes if follow-up measurement had been included. The "consolidation" necessary to benefit from the affective and cognitive processes during intervention not only complicates the picture but provides hints about the process of change. It seems clear that simplistic stimulus-response relationships cannot suffice to describe these patterns of change. The role of internally generated processes must be considerable, possibly indicating that some death intervention programs have such a profound and lasting effect that they cannot be quickly assimilated. Such assimilation takes place in stages, equivalent to mourning (Hardt, 1978–1979) or in succumbing to a terminal illness (Kübler-Ross, 1969).

4. The most surprising findings are those involving an increase in death anxiety. In two out of these three studies, the procedures were primarily didactic. The Wittmaier (1979–1980) program was essentially a course. In the Durlak (1978–1979) study, didactic subjects displayed a large increase, but not the experiential subjects. This increase seemed to result from a presentation to noxious stimuli without the opportunity for "working through." The implications are extremely important in view of the large number of death education courses and various death-related interventions and programs in North America, suggesting that the responsibilities of persons initiating death education or any sort of death intervention efforts

must now be viewed within this context. At one time, psychotherapy was thought to either produce positive effects or none whatsoever. Truax and Carkhoff (1967, p. 5) alerted the psychological community to the possibility that it could turn out to be "for better or for worse." Perhaps the same situation exists whenever we attempt to tamper with a person's death anxiety.

The Zuehlke and Watkins (1975) study was the only one that involved dying persons and the only experientially oriented study that produced a significant increase in death anxiety. These researchers found an increase in purpose-in-life but also an increase in death anxiety following logotherapy for terminal cancer patients. One interpretation of increased death anxiety is that as life took on new meaning, its cessation was perceived as being more negative. An alternative, although not necessarily contradictory, explanation is that the process of denial (or acceptance) that is present in dying patients was interfered with. Regardless of the reasons for the death anxiety increase, the ethical implications, like those for death education and intervention with the healthy, need to be considered.

The increase in death anxiety in some death intervention programs may appear alarming. However, in retrospect, these findings should not seem so strange. Psychologists have long recognized that the presentation of anxiety-fraught stimuli arouses anxiety. The mere presentation of a picture of a snake can be expected to arouse anxiety in those who are afraid of snakes. Boyar (1964), in validating his Fear of Death Scale, predicted and found increased scores after the viewing of a movie on highway accidents. McMordie (1982), in assessing the comparative validity of the true-false DAS and its Likert format (the Templer/McMordie Scale), exposed subjects to death scenarios and found significantly higher scores on both scales than for the control group exposed to a neutral scenario. Therapists/educators/researchers should always assume that death-related stimuli have greater potential to increase rather than decrease death anxiety unless some sort of ingredient for death anxiety reduction is added.

Possibly relevant to the increases in death anxiety following intervention is the recent evidence of a paradoxical increase in general anxiety as a consequence of systematic relaxation training (Heide & Borkovec, 1983). This response has been attributed to the fear of loss of control and a heightening of inward attending or self-confrontation. There is conceivably relevance to death anxiety intervention even beyond those strategies that employ desensitization and other forms of relaxation. It may be that introspection, and the interference with thinking and behavior that function to ward off anxiety, could be especially arousing if either or both are in temporal association with a flooding of death stimuli.

5. Instead of looking at changes in death anxiety in terms of global assessment scores, more attention needs to be paid to fluctuations in the

components making up these scores. A particularly good candidate to examine is the "awareness of the passage of time" component as it is reflected in changes brought about through meditation and near-death experiences. The ability of a person to expand his or her time perspective may prove to be an effective moderator, aiding in the reduction of death anxiety while the foreshortening or compressing of time serves to intensify anxiety.

6. And what about the therapist? Research on the effectiveness of death anxiety therapists, both those who use indirect and direct techniques, may prove very worthwhile. A large number of studies in the 1950s and 1960s demonstrated that "A" therapists, those that relate best to schizophrenics, are more sensitive and intuitive. "B" therapists, those that relate best to neurotics, are more masculine, straightforward, practical, and show interests of a mechanical sort on the Strong Interest Inventory. Perhaps personality variables will, in a similar fashion, identify therapists who work well with strongly death-anxious patients. Our hypothesis is that death anxiety itself will prove to be among the most important of these personality characteristics. Templer, Ruff, and Franks (1971) found considerable death anxiety resemblance in family members, especially husband and wife. "It appears that death anxiety . . . is sensitive to environmental events in general and to the impact of intimate interpersonal relationships in particular." It seems plausible that the death anxiety level of the therapist may have an impact upon the death anxiety level of the patient. Such communication may be of a very subtle sort (e.g., of the nature of "empathic anxiety"), as Sullivan (1953) has described between a mother and her infant. We will go even further and conjecture two-way communication. Perhaps only a very slightly death-anxious therapist can tolerate working all day with strongly death-anxious patients.

Epstein (1979) did, in fact, conduct a study assessing the relationship between analogue therapist personality variables and their relation to response effectiveness. The subjects were undergraduates in an introductory psychology course. They completed a therapeutic effectiveness questionnaire designed to measure the approach-avoidance dimension to death in a simulated therapy situation. Strong death anxiety repressors demonstrated significantly greater avoidance to death-related material then weak death anxiety repressors.

Weinstein (1978) investigated the effects of death anxiety, facilitativeness, and age differential upon the avoidance ("replies to a client's verbal statements which stop or inhibit a client's further expression") of death content by counseling graduate students in a simulated 45-minute session with confederate drama students presenting themselves as terminally ill. Neither facilitativeness score on the Carkhoff Communication

Index nor whether the counselor and client were similar or different in age were related to avoidance. However, there was a trend that approached significance for strongly death-anxious counselors to avoid death content. Further along these lines, Amenta (1984) found that DAS scores were able to predict whether or not hospice volunteers persevered for a year or more or dropped out of the program. Those volunteers who persevered had significantly lower DAS scores upon entering the program, which led Amenta to suggest that death anxiety might prove to be a useful selection/screening technique.

METHODOLOGICAL RECOMMENDATIONS

We would like to recommend that the following points be considered in any assessment of changes in death anxiety resulting from intervention strategies.

1. Follow-up measurements, in addition to measurement before and after a program, are imperative. One may even wish to consider a fourth measurement several months after the previous measurement period. And researchers and therapists should be clear about when to take readings of the criteria and for what purpose.
2. Since death anxiety changes are ordinarily not remarkably large, one wants to avoid a Type II error (i.e., by employing less stringent alpha levels, selecting the appropriate sample size in accordance with power analysis).
3. McMordie's (1978, 1979) seven-point Likert format, instead of the original true-false format of the DAS, may prove to be useful in detecting differences. Although one loses the advantages of norm-like information provided by the many studies that use the original true-false format, the Likert format provides a wider range of inter-item variance. In addition, changes may be reflected more systematically in scales other than the DAS, depending on the nature of the study. For example, Ryan (1982) pointed out that his intervention sessions centered upon the death of loved ones and not on one's own death, which indicated the use of the Collett-Lester Fear of Death of Others and Fear of Dying of Others scales rather than the DAS.
4. Changes in factors scores in addition to changes in total DAS score should be employed (e.g., see Lonetto, Fleming, & Mercer, 1979; Lonetto, 1982).
5. The chances of obtaining decreased death anxiety appear to be greater if the subjects are selected on the basis of having initially high death anxiety. This is not to say that persons with average death anxiety are

not important or that we feel that .05 level of significance is sacrosanct. However, we do see a need to map out the broad parameters of death anxiety interventions in the next few years before proceeding on to the variables that carry potentially less impact.

6. Control groups should be employed. This is not to say that the previous studies without control groups are without value. We believe that death anxiety ordinarily does not have dramatic spontaneous or environmentally induced changes within a period of a few days or weeks. In fact, almost all the control groups in the intervention studies we reviewed did not significantly change in DAS score. Nevertheless, control groups do increase the certainty of one's inferences, especially when the research combines both factor and total scale scores.
7. It would be well to determine not only changes in mean death anxiety scores but also changes in standard deviations. Spencer (1976) found that although persons who had been involved in near-death accidents did not differ in their mean anxiety scores, they had significantly greater standard deviations. The singular pronouncement of nonsignificance in intervention programs could obscure meaningful changes in individual subjects. Therefore, both *intra*individual changes and *inter*individual changes should be examined.

6

CONCLUDING THOUGHTS

In the imagery of Zen, a student is likened to a mosquito biting an iron bull, or to a man who has swallowed a red-hot iron which he can neither spit out nor gulp down.

(Alan Watts, *Psychotherapy East and West*, 1975, p. 165)

At times we may feel like a student of Zen as we try to follow the many threads of death anxiety. It does not behave or respond to social, personal, or environmental factors in the same way as do better-documented forms of anxiety. Not only does death anxiety react differently, it refuses to be bound by unidimensional definitions. In fact, death anxiety is a compound of at least four distinct components.

1. Concern about intellectual and personal emotional reactions to death
2. Concern about physical change
3. Awareness of and concern about the passage of time
4. Concern about the pain and stress that can accompany illness and dying

These components reflect a need to understand and cope with loss and change, whether they be internal or external, and to embrace the very movements of perceived time. This compelling mixture of concerns is also related to what a number of theorists and practitioners believe to be our most basic anxiety, the fear of separation. In the highly dramatic and radical change that birth signifies are the roots not only of fear of separation but also of other anxieties—of change, the aftermath of change, of life after death, and of death itself.

The evidence and ideas presented in this book strongly suggest that change and death anxiety have shared a long history and will continue to do so. Death anxiety cannot be adequately assessed without an understanding of this relationship. Tuned to the sense of flow in our lives, death anxiety can take on a uniquely personal pattern of highs and lows. It can, at the same time, serve as a guide for the course of a person's life or of the society she or he lives in. Death anxiety may be more than a guide; it may be an integral part of the flow of life itself. In this way, it can be thought of as a river that begins in the first moments of existence in the world, which later empties into a great sea of memories, experiences, and symbols with our death. Calm, effortlessly moving, or cascading over treacherous rocks, death anxiety continues on, propelled by thoughts, feelings, and actions and in turn providing these aspects of our lives with the energy to survive.

The concept of a lifelong, altering and active form of anxiety is hardly what might be called traditional. But death anxiety defies tradition by focusing in on experiential and symbolic factors while resisting the fertile ground of biographic and personality variables. Death anxiety shows a preference for the humanistic and existential (i.e., imagery, perceptions of physical, spiritual and mental change, and of the environment), and we certainly need to explore the full scope of its relationships to these intriguing positions about the human condition.

> *Death imagery has undergone a significant and overlooked shift from the long-held image of death as a macabre figure to one of death as a gay deceiver or gentle comforter. The importance of this shift is that these latter images have the potential to alter anxiety about death.*
>
> *"The troubles," as the civil disturbances are called in Northern Ireland, have become associated with fears of "getting cancer." One, in fact, has become a symbol for the other, and both are related to concerns about the pain and stress brought about by illness and dying. (Lonetto, 1982)*

These examples and others provided in Chapter 4 demonstrate that death anxiety and imagery about death form a vital link between our perceptions of crises and how well we cope. There are no clearer examples than those found in Lifton's (1965) study of the survivors of Hiroshima and Torrance's (1958) work on battle fatigue.

The reluctance death anxiety has displayed to being pigeonholed by conservative methodologies is relatively minor compared to its ability to defend itself against a variety of intervention strategies. By and large, programs relying solely on didactic procedures have failed to (1) recognize the blending of idiosyncratic and common properties of death anxiety and (2) control or manage anxiety. In contrast, experientially based programs, which are just learning how to tap into the dynamics of death anxiety, show much more promise.

However, both approaches share similar problems—how and when should changes in anxiety be measured? If we conceive of death anxiety as a flowing river to be assessed at a number of locations along its course, then is change an alteration in its flow? In its direction? In its intensity? Or in its consequences? At the present time, studies on death anxiety have reached into many personal rivers at many locations; now we have to learn how to utilize these assessments. We have to learn how to develop more experience-based programs to match and regulate the movements of death anxiety. We feel that at some point, intervention programs must be thought of and accepted as rituals that allow death anxiety a form of expression and release. In the meantime, questions of how much death anxiety is necessary for survival are waiting to be answered.

Do high levels of anxiety lead to a paralysis of meaningful activities of the simple routines of everyday life? A returning Vietnam vet, who had witnessed the death of his friends during a mortar attack, refused to leave his house at night. His wife and children were not all allowed out at the same time. Someone had to stay behind. During the day, he would drive his newly purchased Trans Am but never over 35 mph, even on the highway. This went on for more than two years before his life went back to being normal. Only his dreams were a reminder of the war.

Do extremely low levels of anxiety lead to an increase in risk-taking behaviors, even to the point of being life-threatening? We know that soldiers who have spent too many hours in combat run the risk of being too careless and reckless.

Are our children's worries about nuclear war a reflection of significant changes in their anxiety about their own death—and that of their friends and parents—and their anxiety about their future? Do our ideas about immortality surface as death anxiety rises? Or, does death anxiety act as a fluctuating barrier between beliefs about survival and personal immortality?

In one sense these questions, as serious as they sound, underscore a misunderstanding of the historical importance of death anxiety. This anxiety, by its very nature, helps us to survive. It also gives us a feeling of continuity because it has always been inseparable from the human condition. This often elusive, constant, and timeless companion permits us to remain in contact with the past and present while we anticipate our future.

Yet, in another sense these are questions that haunt us, and will continue to, until we begin to piece together the various parts of the riddle with which death anxiety has presented us. This book is a compendium of quantitative, philosophical, and psychological information about death anxiety to help solve the riddle. It is such a fascinating task to study a variable that is so basic and mysterious. Are there many other variables that can bring us closer to finding one of the keys to our own humanity?

When our life has lost the sense of meaning, when life's spiral seems to be unraveling, we come to know death anxiety. When our life is filled with an inner calmness and certainty, we know this anxiety as well. It is there, unfelt, an ally.

APPENDIX

THE MEASUREMENT OF DEATH ANXIETY

Asking

Words of Buddha:

Imagine a man that has been pierced by an arrow well soaked in poison, and his relatives and friends go at once to fetch a physician or a surgeon. Imagine now that this man says:

"I will not have this arrow pulled out until I know the name of the man who shot it, and the name of his family, and whether he is tall or short or of medium height; until I know whether he is black or dark or yellow; until I know his village or town. I will not have the arrow pulled out until I know the bow that shot it, whether it was a long bow or a cross bow.

"I will not have this arrow pulled out until I know about the bow-string, and the arrow, and the feathers of the arrow, whether they are feathers of vulture, or kite or peacock.

"I will not have this arrow pulled out until I know whether the tendon which binds it is of an ox, or deer, or monkey.

"I will not have this arrow pulled out until I know whether it is an arrow, or the edge of a knife, or a splinter, or the tooth of a calf, or the head of a javelin."

Well, that man would die, but he would die without having found out all these things.

(Majjhima Nikaya, *Lamps of Fire,* 1961, p. 164)

At the time of the construction of the DAS in the mid 1960s, the most salient methodological deficiency in studies and observations of death anxiety was the lack of psychometrically defined instruments for measuring such anxiety. Much of the material that had appeared in the literature was based upon clinical impression or armchair speculation. More importantly, the less subjective methods of assessing death anxiety have not had their reliability and validity adequately determined.

A number of the interviews used were loosely structured (Schilder & Wechsler, 1934; Caprio, 1950; Cummings & Henry, 1961; Hackett & Weisman, 1965), while other researchers employed a scientific set of questions (Scott, 1896; Bromberg & Schilder, 1938, 1939; Schilder, 1936; Chandler, 1950; Feifel, 1955; Feifel, 1956; Christ, 1961; Jeffers, Nichols, & Eisdorfer, 1961). These interviews ranged from the lengthy 32 questions of Bromberg and Schilder to the simply worded and straightforward questions of Jeffers et al. The latter investigators asked, "Are you afraid to die?" and "Do you believe in life after death?"

Researchers also tended to employ conventional projective instruments. Rhudick and Dibner (1961) defined death concern as the introduction of death into a TAT story, and rated each story with death concern from 1 to 3 points, depending upon the usual frequency of a death theme for that card as determined by a pilot study. Shrut (1958) administered the TAT and a Sentence Completion Test to a group of elderly people, reporting only that clinical impressions were utilized, and offering no description of the criteria or method of quantification of responses.

McCully (1963) asked children to make up stories, Mauer (1964) required high school students to write essays on "What comes to mind when I think of death"; while Faunce and Fulton (1958) administered incomplete sentences with death involved items to college students. Corey (1961) utilized a procedure in which a picture of a reclining figure was presented to subjects who were supposed to specify whether the figure was "sleeping" or "dead." On the second presentation, the subjects were instructed to say whether the figure was "lifeless" or "napping."

Most questionnaire and checklist assessments have been rather brief (Sarnoff & Corwin, 1959; Diggory & Rothman, 1961; Swenson, 1961; Dickstein, 1976), while others were fairly extensive (Middleton, 1936; Stacey, Chalmers, & Markin, 1952; Kalish, 1963), including the work of Means (1936) who had college women rate the extent to which several hundred objects and ideas evoked fear in them, with only a small percentage of the items pertaining to death.

BOYAR'S FEAR OF DEATH SCALE

Jerome Boyar's dissertation (unpublished), written in 1964 for the University of Rochester, details the development of his Fear of Death Scale (FODS). It was clearly more sophisticated than any of the instruments used to measure death anxiety up until that time. Boyar obtained an initial pool of items on the basis of individual interviews. He then had judges rate the adequacy of his items. Next, the items were embedded in filler items, split-half reliability was determined, and item-item and item-test correlations were computed. To test the validity of the FODS, subjects completed the Scale before and after a movie on highway accidents intended to increase their anxiety. Since the FODS scores for this experimental group increased to a significantly greater extent than did those of the control group shown a relatively innocuous movie, Boyer concluded that the validity of his scale was established (Table A.1 lists the 18 FODS items).

Although Boyar's FODS seemed to be more adequate than any other death fear instrument, the reservations about it pertained to items related to the act of dying, the finality of death, corpses, and burial. That is, the content of the scale did not reflect a wide variety of life experiences. Also,

TABLE A.1 List of 18 FODS Items Included in Validity Experiment

1. Graveyards seem to upset many people but they do not bother me.
2. The idea of never thinking again after I die frightens me.
3. The idea that I may die young does not affect me.
4. The feeling that I will be missing out on so much after I die disturbs me.
5. I do not mind the idea of being shut into a coffin when I die.
6. Some people are afraid to die, but I am not.
7. The pain involved in dying frightens me.
8. The idea of being buried frightens me.
9. Not knowing what it feels like to die makes me anxious.
10. I am not afraid of a long, slow dying.
11. I have moments when I get really upset about dying.
12. Coffins make me anxious.
13. Being totally immobile after death bothers me.
14. Never again feeling anything when I die upsets me.
15. The sight of a corpse does not make me at all anxious.
16. I am not at all disturbed by the finality of death.
17. The total isolation of death is frightening to me.
18. What will happen to my body after death does not concern me.

any attempt to establish construct validity by a diversity of procedures was less exhaustive than the procedures employed by Templer with his Death Anxiety Scale (DAS).

In addition to the DAS and Boyar's Fear of Death Scale, other death attitude scales have been developed. However, a good deal of the research described in this book focused on the DAS. This was for the purpose of consistency in that the DAS was, and continues to be, the most widely used of the death fear instruments and has more validation and accumulation of published material than the others (i.e., McMordie, 1978). However, for certain specific purposes, one of the other scales may be the instrument of choice. For example, the Collett-Lester Fear of Death Scale has two subscales that assess one's fear of other persons' death and dying.

OTHER DEATH ATTITUDE SCALES*

Collett-Lester Fear of Death Scale

The Collett-Lester Fear of Death Scale (Collett & Lester, 1969) has four scales that provide a separate score for fear of death of oneself, fear of death of others, fear of dying of oneself, and fear of dying of others. The 36 items are in a six-point format from "strong agreement" to "strong disagreement." Factor analysis has revealed that as many as 11 factors, with the first factor corresponding to fear of death of self and the second factor (Factor II) to fear of dying of others. The other factors describe a mixture of such fears.

Dickstein's Death Concern Scale

Dickstein's (1972) Death Concern Scale is a 30-item, four-point scale that assesses the extent that an individual consciously contemplates death and evaluates it negatively. Factor analyses have shown a Conscious Contemplation Factor and a Negative Evaluation Factor (Klug & Boss, 1976, 1977). DAS total scale scores were found to correlate more highly with the Negative Evaluation Factor than with the Conscious Contemplation Factor.

Lester's Attitude Toward Death Scale

Lester's (1967a) Attitude Toward Death Scale consists of 21 statements to which the respondent agrees or disagrees. Each statement has a value that

*Although Handal's Death Anxiety Scale, Lester's Fear of Death Scale, Day and Najman's Death Acceptance Scale, and Sarnoff and Corwin's Fear of Death Scale are also available, their range of application has not been as great as the scales described in the text.

indicates how favorable it is as an expression of an attitude toward death. As examples, the item stating that "the dead are eternally happy in heaven" has a value of 2.00 and the item that "death is the worse thing that could happen" has a value of 10.76. In addition to the total score indicating overall attitude toward death, there is a score indicating the degree of inconsistency in the subject's attitudes toward death. There are parallel forms of the scale.

Nelson and Nelson Scale

Nelson and Nelson's (1975) scale consists of 24 Likert-format items. They seem to have a flavor similar to the items of the DAS. In fact, two of them are identical—"I am very much afraid to die" and "It does not make me nervous when people talk about death." Three others are quite similar. Nelson and Nelson reported that four factors—Death Avoidance, Death Fear, Death Denial, and Reluctance to Interact with the Dying—account for the major contribution to the variance of the scale.

Kreiger, Epsting, and Leitner's Threat Index

The Threat Index (Kreiger, Epsting, & Leitner, 1974) is based on George Kelly's theory of personal constructs. Individuals are presented triads of cards drawn from cards with death related statements. They place the elements "preferred self," "self," and "my own death" on either a construct or contrast pole for each statement. The Death Threat score is the number of times "my own death" is placed on a different pole from "self" and "preferred self."

MMPI Death Anxiety Scale

Templer and Lester (1974) attempted to construct an MMPI scale assessing death anxiety by correlating MMPI with DAS items, but only nine items survived cross-validation. The authors stated, "The content of the nine MMPI items appears to pertain to introversion, worry, anxiety, a concern about sickness and pain, and lack of self-confidence." In fact, three of the nine items are also Manifest Anxiety Scale items. Although this study can probably be regarded as a failure to produce a useful MMPI death anxiety scale, confirmation of a general relationship between death anxiety and general maladjustment and psychopathology was provided.

THE DEATH ANXIETY SCALE (DAS)

The first step in the construction of the DAS (1967, 1969, 1970) was to devise 40 items that on a rational basis seemed to describe death anxiety as it is reflected in a wide variety of life experiences and to broaden the intent of Boyar's Fear of Death Scale (see Table A.2).

The next step was the determination of the face validity of these 40 items by the judgment of a clinical psychologist, two clinical psychology graduate students, and four chaplains in a state hospital. These judges rated each item from one to five on this basis: (1) irrelevant to death anxiety, (2) slightly associated with death anxiety, (3) moderately associated with death

TABLE A.2 The Initial Pool of 40 Death Anxiety Scale (DAS) Items

Number	Key	Item
1	T	I am a little melancholy when my birthday comes around.
2	T	I am very much afraid to die.
3	F	I'm not afraid of growing old.
4	T	I think about death every day.
5	F	The thought of death seldom enters my mind.
6	T	It upsets me to read about famous people who pass away.
7	F	Attending a funeral of a friend doesn't bother my nerves too much.
8	T	I feel a bit of sadness when the leaves drop from the trees in the fall.
9	F	It doesn't make me nervous when people talk about death.
10	T	I dread to think about having to have an operation.
11	F	I am not at all afraid to die.
12	F	I am not particularly afraid of getting cancer.
13	T	I firmly believe that many more shelters should be built in case of an atom bomb attack.
14	F	I don't worry excessively about something happening to my loved ones.
15	T	I hate to think about dogs and cats being killed, even for research purposes.
16	F	I have few fears about riding in an airplane.
17	T	It makes me feel ill at ease when someone even mentions the word "death."
18	F	The thought of death never bothers me.
19	T	I very much want to lead a very long life, at least 90 years.
20	T	I get an uncomfortable feeling as soon as I walk into a hospital.
21	T	When I was a child, I dwelled more upon death than most youngsters.
22	F	Passing by cemeteries doesn't particularly bother me.
23	T	I am often distressed by the way time flies so very rapidly.

TABLE A.2 The Initial Pool of 40 Death Anxiety Scale (DAS) Items (*Continued*)

Number	Key	Item
24	T	I fear dying a painful death.
25	F	I have a philosophy of life that permits me to be reconciled to my mortality.
26	T	The subject of life after death troubles me greatly.
27	T	I am really scared of having a heart attack.
28	F	I like to watch murder mystery programs on television.
29	F	I'm not particularly afraid of high places.
30	T	I often think about how short life really is.
31	T	I don't like to see candles slowly burn out.
32	T	It distresses me to read about the plagues and horrible diseases of the Middle Ages.
33	T	I shudder when I hear people talking about a World War III.
34	F	I have never worried about burglars and prowlers as I lay in bed at night.
35	T	The sight of a dead body is horrifying to me.
36	F	The sight of blood doesn't affect me much.
37	T	I am made uncomfortable by looking at a crucifix in a church.
38	T	At one time in my life I was afraid of ghosts.
39	F	I feel that the future holds nothing for me to fear.
40	F	I'm not afraid of germs.

anxiety, (4) considerably associated with death anxiety, and (5) very greatly associated with death anxiety. The average rating for each item was then calculated. Nine items received an average rating of below 3.0 and were discarded. The 31 remaining items were embedded in 200 filler items—the last 200 items of the Minnesota Multiphasic Personality Inventory (MMPI).

Internal consistency was determined by using item-total score point biserial correlation coefficients for the 31 items retained for three independent groups of subjects: (1) 45 college students in a sophomore undergraduate psychology class in the University of Kentucky, (2) 50 college students from age 25 to 57 in a number of different classes in several different colleges in Kentucky and Tennessee, and (3) 46 students in an introductory psychology class at Western Kentucky University. It was decided to retain those items that had point biserial coefficients significant at the .10 level in two out of three analyses. Table A.3 contains the 15 retained items which constitute the DAS.

It is noteworthy that the 15 items that survived both the face validity and the internal consistency analyses tend to be of a very direct sort. The more

TABLE A.3 The Death Anxiety Scale (DAS)

1.	T	I am very much afraid to die.
2.	F	The thought of death seldom enters my mind.
3.	F	It doesn't make me nervous when people talk about death.
4.	T	I dread to think about having to have an operation.
5.	F	I am not at all afraid to die.
6.	F	I am not particularly afraid of getting cancer.
7.	F	The thought of death never bothers me.
8.	T	I am often distressed by the way time flies so very rapidly.
9.	T	I fear dying a painful death.
10.	T	The subject of life after death troubles me greatly.
11.	T	I am really scared of having a heart attack.
12.	T	I often think about how short life really is.
13.	T	I shudder when I hear people talking about a World War III.
14.	T	The sight of a dead body is horrifying to me.
15.	F	I feel that the future holds nothing for me to fear.

remote and abtruse items such as "I don't like to see candles slowly burn out" were discarded.

Phi coefficients were computed as a means of determining interitem correlations. As only 20 of the 315 phi coefficients between the retained items exceeded .40, it can be inferred that there is not excessive interitem redundancy.

Reliability

Thirty-one of the 37 Hopkinsville Community College students who participated in the agreement response set research, described below, completed the DAS a second time, three weeks after the first administration. The product-moment correlation between these two sets of scores of .83 demonstrated satisfactory test-retest reliability. A coefficient of .76 (Kuder-Richardson Formula 20) demonstrated reasonable internal consistency with these same subjects.

Response Sets

Nine of the 15 items that comprise the DAS are keyed "true" and six are keyed "false." To determine whether or not the DAS is appreciably related to agreement response set, it was correlated with the 15 items that Couch and Keniston (1960) considered the best short-scale measure of agreeing response tendency. For 37 students at Hopkinsville (Kentucky) Community College, the product-moment correlation coefficient was .23 (NS). This result demonstrated that agreement response set accounted for little of the variance of the DAS.

The DAS and the Marlowe-Crowne Social Desirability Scale (Crowne & Marlowe, 1960) were completed by 46 Introductory Psychology students at Western Kentucky University. The product-moment correlation coefficient between the two scales was not significant ($r = .03$). It appeared then that the response set of social desirability was not appreciably related to the death anxiety variable. However, subsequent research does seem to indicate a slight negative relationship between the DAS and social desirability (Dickstein, 1977–1978; McMordie, 1978; Durlak, 1978–1979; Martin, 1982–1983; Handal, Peal, Napoli, & Austrin, 1984–1985).

Validation Procedures

In an effort to establish the construct validity (Cronbach & Meehl, 1955) of the DAS, two separate projects were undertaken. In the first, the subjects were psychiatric patients in a state mental hospital; in the second, the subjects were college students.

1. DAS Scores of High-Death-Anxiety Patients and Controls

The DAS scores of 21 presumably high-death-anxiety psychiatric patients were compared with those of control patients. The patients drawn from Western State Hospital in Hopkinsville, Kentucky, had spontaneously verbalized fear of or preoccupation with death and were enlisted by (1) referrals by hospital chaplains who had been told of death anxiety in counseling sessions, (2) a list of names obtained form the director of nursing by consulting with her professional nursing staff, and (3) patients' records. The control subjects were matched for diagnosis, sex, and approximate age. Table A.4 lists the DAS scores and other pertinent information about each patient used in the study. The 21 high-death-anxiety subjects had a DAS mean of 11.62 and the control group obtained a mean of 6.77 ($t = 5.78$, $p < .01$), indicating that psychiatric patients who spontaneously verbalize death anxiety concern have higher DAS scores than other psychiatric patients.

TABLE A.4 DAS Score of High-Death-Anxiety Patients and Controls

High-death-anxiety patients					Control patients				
Patients	Sex	Age	Diagnosis	DAS score	Patients	Sex	Age	Diagnosis	DAS score
1-A	M	24	P	12	1-B	M	21	P	6
2-A	M	21	S	14	2-B	M	24	S	12
3-A	M	25	S	6	3-B	M	21	S	3
4-A	M	62	P	11	4-B	M	60	P	9
5-A	M	66	MD-D	14	5-B	M	64	IPR	10
6-A	M	49	S	9	6-B	M	41	S	10
7-A	F	27	P	15	7-B	F	21	P	4
8-A	F	26	N	11	8-B	F	37	N	5
9-A	F	46	N	11	9-B	F	45	N	7
10-A	F	41	S	12	10-B	F	36	S	6
11-A	F	49	S	9	11-B	F	46	S	4
12-A	F	36	S	9	12-B	F	38	S	8
13-A	F	56	MD-D	15	13-B	F	55	MD-D	10
14-A	F	36	N	18	14-B	F	31	N	4
15-A	F	24	N	13	15-B	F	30	N	8
16-A	F	74	S	13	16-B	F	72	S	6
17-A	F	35	N	14	17-B	F	37	N	7
18-A	M	32	P	10	18-B	M	38	P	6
19-A	M	28	S	11	19-B	M	21	S	2
20-A	F	24	S	8	20-B	F	28	S	8
21-A	F	41	S	14	21-B	F	41	S	7

Note: S, schizophrenia; P, personality disorder; IPR, involutional psychotic reaction; N, neurosis; MD-D, manic depressive–depressed type.

2. *The DAS Score Correlates of College Students*

The DAS, Boyar's Fear of Death Scale (FODS), and the MMPI were administered to 77 undergraduates at Murray State University. Thirty-nine of the subjects were drawn from a class in educational psychology and 38 were enrolled in a course in experimental psychology. After the students completed the first 366 items of the MMPI, they were given a 15-minute break. In the second part of the session, the students were given the DAS (15 items of which are embedded in the last 200 items of the MMPI), and the FODS.

Boyar's FODS was employed as one means of determining the construct validity of the DAS, although the construct validity of Boyar's FODS had not been definitively established. The utilization of a measure of questionable validity as an adjunct to establishing the validity of a given test is what Cronbach and Meehl (1955) have referred to as the "bootstraps effect."

The MMPI was employed for two reasons. First, the MMPI contains three well-known anxiety scales, the Manifest Anxiety Scale (Taylor, 1951), the Welsh Anxiety Scale (Welsh, 1956a), and the Welsh Anxiety Index (Welsh, 1956b). If the DAS correlated as highly with these scales as they correlate with one another, then it could be argued that the DAS measures anxiety in general rather than death anxiety in particular. The scale would then not have what Campbell (1960) has termed discriminant validity. On the other hand, modest positive correlations with scales of general anxiety were predicted since such has been the case with other specific scales of anxiety. The second reason for the utilization of the MMPI was that it was considered worthwhile to determine the relationship of the DAS to personality variables. The correlations with the clinical and validity scales will be discussed later in the section on the MMPI and anxiety.

Table A.5 presents the product-moment correlation coefficients between the DAS and the other variables. The correlation of .74 between the DAS and the FODS was regarded as surprisingly high. Furthermore, the FODS correlations with other variables parallel very closely those for the DAS. Although it was anticipated that the DAS would be more independent of the FODS in view of the different rationale and item content, the fact that the high relationship was found provides mutual evidence for the validity of both scales.

The product-moment correlation coefficients between the DAS, the Manifest Anxiety Scale, and the Welsh Anxiety Scale are .39 and .36, respectively ($p < .05$). The DAS correlation coefficient with the Welsh Anxiety Index ($r = .18$) was not significant. In general, it can be said that death anxiety correlates positively with general anxiety, although not as highly as the intercorrelations among scales of general anxiety themselves,

TABLE A.5 Correlations of DAS with MMPI Variables for College Students (N = 76)

Variable	Correlation with DAS
FODS (N = 70)	.74**
L	.05
F	.13
K	—.43**
Hs	—.04
D	.03
Hy	—.01
Pd	—.24*
Mf	—.14
Pa	—.09
Pt	.04
Sc	—.08
Ma	.12
Si	.25*
Welsh Anxiety Scale	.39**
Welsh Anxiety Index	.18
Manifest Anxiety Scale	.36**
Emotional words (N = 77)	.25*

*Significant at .05 level.
**Significant at .01 level.

and not nearly as highly as the .74 correlation obtained with Boyar's FODS. The DAS does possess discriminant validity, and it cannot be said that the DAS is just another measure of general anxiety.

In terms of the relationship between DAS total scale scores and other death-related assessments, the correlations reported are "to be expected" in view of the differences in the aims and scaling of the assessments (see Table A.6). Significant correlations ranged from .23, with the Dying of Others subscale of the Collett-Lester Fear of Death Scale (percentage of variance accounted for = 5.29 percent) to a high of .81 with Boyar's FODS (percentage of variance accounted for = 65.61 percent). It is also worthwhile to note that the DAS showed the highest correlations with the FODS.

To Embed or Not to Embed

In the construction and validation of the DAS, the items were embedded in the last 200 items of the MMPI. The embedded DAS format greatly extends

TABLE A.6 Correlations of Other Death-Related Assessments with Death Anxiety Scale

	Study													
	Abdel-Khalek (personal communication, 1985)	Bailis & Kennedy (1977)	Handal et al. (1984–1985)	Holmes & Anderson (1980)	Klug & Boss (1977)	Kuperman & Golden (1978)	Lattamer & Hayslip (1984–1985)	McDonald & Carroll (1981)	Neimeyer (1980–1981)	Ochs (1979)	Slezak (1979, 1980)	Templer (1967, 1969, 1970)	Vargo (1980)	Warren (1981–1982)
Boyar's Fear of Death Scale				.81								.74		
Collett-Lester Fear of Death Scale (total score)	.72	.66 & .55												
Death of self	.54						.54		.52		.59		.61	
Death of others	.55						.35		.56		.48		.52	
Dying of self	.52						.42		.53		.59		.43	
Dying of others	.56						.27		.23		.29		.40	
Dickstein's Death Concern Scale (total score)						.67	.55			.62 & .69				.42
Factor I					.42 & .49									
Factor II					.68 & .60									
Handal's Death Anxiety Scale								.50						
Livingston & Zimet Death Anxiety Scale			.64											
Lester Fear of Death Scale									.32					
Nelson & Nelson's Scale				.66										
Kreiger et al. Threat Index														.10*
Ray & Najman Death Acceptance Scale														—.36
Sarnoff & Cowin's Fear of Death Scale														.39

*Not significant.

administration time when the filler items have no other use, and this is a disadvantage in research requiring a large number of volunteer subjects.

In order to determine if the embedding of the items has an effect upon the DAS score, the DAS was administered to 158 students at Hopkinsville (Kentucky) Community College (Templer & Ruff, 1971). The items were embedded for 78 participants, 30 males and 48 females and not embedded for 80 participants, 32 males and 48 females. (The embedded items were placed in the last 200 items of the MMPI.) For the nonembedded DAS, items were placed before the 200 MMPI items, so that both groups would complete questionnaires in approximately equal time and thereby obtain the impression that they were working on identical material. The embedded and nonembedded DASs were given to every other participant.

The DAS means were 7.08 and 7.30 for the embedded and nonembedded administrations, respectively (t = .45, NS), while the variances were 11.29 and 7.58 (F = 1.49, $p < .05$).

Since there did not appear to be any readily apparent explanation for the significant difference in variance, replication was carried out to rule out a type-I error. The DAS was administered in a similar fashion to 186 different students at Hopkinsville Community College. The DAS mean for the 93 participants with the DAS items embedded was 6.70; that for the 93 participants with the items not embedded was 6.95 (t = 50, NS), with variances of 11.76 and 10.79 (F = 1.09, NS). A reasonable conclusion was that the embedding of DAS items has little or no effect upon scores. In almost all DAS research subsequent to the development of the DAS, the items have not been embedded.

Likert Format

McMordie (1979, 1982) and McMordie and Kumar (1984) developed a seven-point Likert version of the DAS which was called the Templer/McMordie Scale. The response alternatives range from "very strongly agree" to "very strongly disagree," with a neutral midvalue category. An undecided response category was also offered. "Scores for undecided responses are assigned by substituting the mean rounded-off to the nearest whole number for items not answered with an undecided response." In addition, McMordie constructed a Templer/McMordie II Scale with the wording of the items changed to a greater intensity level by changing qualifiers and making the items more personal. For example, "not particularly afraid" was changed to "scares me greatly;" and "the thought of death" was changed to the "thought of my death."

A comparison of the original true-false DAS, the Templer/McMordie Scale, and the Templer/McMordie II Scale by McMordie (1982) revealed that for the DAS, an internal consistency coefficient of .76 was found, which parallels the value originally reported by Templer. However, an internal consistency coefficient of .84 was obtained with both of the Templer/McMordie scales. In this study the DAS correlated .85 with the Templer/McMordie and .77 with the Templer/McMordie II. Although McMordie failed to demonstrate significantly greater validity for the

TABLE A.7 DAS Means and Standard Deviations in Various Studies

	Subjects	M	SD
134	Lincoln University undergraduate blacks (Pandey & Templer, 1972)	6.35	3.28
124	Lincoln University undergraduate whites (Templer, 1969, 1970)	6.16	3.21
77	Murray University undergraduates	5.13	3.10
32	Heterogeneous psychiatric patients	6.78	2.97
21	High-death-anxiety psychiatric patients	11.62	1.96
21	Controls for high-death-anxiety psychiatric patients (Templer & Dotson, 1970)	6.77	2.74
104	Male Western Kentucky University undergraduates	6.07	3.12
109	Female Western Kentucky University undergraduates (Templer, Ruff, & Franks, 1971)	6.66	3.07
123	Male apartment house residents	4.85	2.88
160	Female apartment house residents	6.11	3.31
299	Adolescent males	5.72	3.07
444	Adolescent females	6.84	3.21
569	Fathers of adolescents	5.74	3.32
702	Mothers of adolescents	6.43	3.22
78	Male heterogeneous psychiatric patients	6.50	3.55
59	Female heterogeneous psychiatric patients	7.15	3.72
13	Male psychiatric aides	5.08	2.25
112	Female psychiatric aides (Templer, 1971a)	6.33	3.24
49	Heterogeneous psychiatric patients (Templer, 1971b)	7.13	3.45
46	Retired males	4.15	3.29
29	Retired females (Templer, 1972)	4.41	3.43
217	Bloomfield (N.J.) college males	6.69	2.72
167	Bloomfield (N.J.) college females	7.84	2.99

TABLE A.8 Means and Standard Deviations for Death Anxiety Scale*

	Youth		Young adult		Middle-aged		Elderly		Total	
	M	SD	M	SD	M	SD	M	SD	M	SD
Males	7.73	3.59	6.87	3.04	6.61	2.92	4.91	2.79	6.55	3.22
Females	7.43	3.64	7.42	2.79	7.02	2.67	6.16	2.97	7.06	3.19
Total	7.50	3.61	7.25	2.85	6.85	2.77	5.74	2.95	6.89	3.10

*Reported by Stevens, Cooper, & Thomas, 1980.

Templer/McMordie Scale over the DAS,* the former scale may still prove to be especially useful when the sensitivity to detect change over time is important.

Normlike Information

Although comprehensive representative norms have not been established, a number of means and standard deviations have been reported. Templer and Ruff (1971) presented the means and standard deviations for 23 categories of subjects from seven different studies involving over 3,600 adults and adolescents (see Table A.7). Templer and Ruff stated that "Means of normal S tend to be roughly from 4.5 to 7.0; the standard deviation a little over 3.0. Psychiatric patients obtained higher scores than normals. Females consistently have higher DAS scores than males." Stevens, Cooper, and Thomas (1980) presented normative information based upon a cross-sectional sample of 295 middle-class persons in Connecticut (see Table A.8). The mean reported was 7.50 for youths, 7.25 for young adults, 6.85 for the middle-aged, and 5.75 for the elderly. The overall mean was 6.89 (SD = 3.20), 6.55 for males and 7.06 for females. The decreasing means with age reported by Stevens et al. is in line with the small inverse correlations found between age and death anxiety (see Chapter 2).

Although the DAS meets the accepted standards for a paper-and-pencil assessment technique, questions arise in connection with further partitioning total DAS scores into systematically appearing components (see Chapter 3), and the relationship of total and component scores to a representative sampling of internal and external variables (Chapters 3, 4, and 5).

**Non-English translations*: Although the vast majority of the DAS research has been conducted in predominantly English-speaking countries, the DAS has been translated into Arabic (Beshai & Templer, 1978; Abdel-Khalek, personal communication, 1985), German (Witkowski & Baumgartner, 1977), Spanish (Caro & Campos, 1980), Hindi (Mukhopadhyay, personal communication, 1980), Chinese (Ulim, personal communication, 1985), Korean (Young Sook Joo, personal communication, 1983), Afrikaans (Poss, personal communication, 1973), and Japanese (Ohyama, Furuta, & Hatayama, 1978).

REFERENCES

Aday, R. H. (1984–1985). Belief in afterlife and death anxiety: Correlates and comparisons, *Omega, 15,* 67–75.

Adler, A. (1927). *The individual psychology of Alfred Adler,* H. L. Ansbach and R. Ansbacher (Eds.). New York: Basic Books.

Agras, S. (1959). The relationship of school phobia to childhood depression. *American Journal of Psychiatry, 116,* 533–536.

Alcorn, H. G. (1976). *The relationship between death anxiety and self-esteem.* United States International University, unpublished doctoral dissertation.

Alexander, I. E., & Adlerstein, A. M. (1958). Affective responses to the concept of death in a population of children and early adolescents. *Journal of General Psychology, 93,* 167–177.

Alexander, I. E., Colley, R. S., & Adlerstein, A. M. (1957). Is death a matter of indifference? *Journal of Psychology, 43,* 277–283.

Alpers, B. J. (1950). *Clinical neurology.* Philadelphia: Davis.

Amenta, M. M. (1984). Death anxiety, purpose in life and duration of service in hospice volunteers. *Psychological Reports, 54,* 979–984.

Anthony, S. 1940. *The child's discovery of death.* New York: Harcourt, Brace and World.

Anthony, S. (1973). *The discovery of death in childhood and after.* Hammondsworth, Middlesex: Penguin Education.

Aries, P. (1974). *Western attitude toward death from the Middle Ages to the present.* Baltimore: John Hopkins University Press.

Aring, C. (1968). Intimations of mortality: An appreciation of death and dying. *Annals of Internal Medicine,* 737–752.

Arndt, K. S. (1982). *The measure of death anxiety on college students in regard to selected variables.* Eastern College, unpublished master's thesis.

Aronow, E., Rauchway, A., Peller, M., & Devito, A. (1980–1981). The value of the self in relation to fear of death. *Omega, 11,* 37–44.

Bahnson, E. (1965). Emotional reactions to internally and externally derived threat of annihilation. In F. H. Grosser, H. Wechsler, & M. Greenblat (Eds.), *The threat of impending disaster: Contribution to a psychology of stress.* Cambridge, MA: The MIT Press.

Bailis, L. A., & Kennedy, W. R. (1977). Effects of a death education program upon secondary school students. *Journal of Educational Research, 71,* 63-66.

Bakshis, R. et al. (1974). "Meanings" toward death: A TST strategy. *Omega, 5,* 161-177.

Barron, F. (1956). An ego strength scale which predicts response to psychotherapy. In G. G. Welsh & W. G. Dahlstrom (Eds.), *Basic readings on the MMPI in psychology and medicine.* Minneapolis: University of Minnesota Press.

Bascue, L. O. (1973). *A study of the relationship of time orientation and time attitude to death anxiety in elderly people.* Unpublished doctoral dissertation, University of Maryland, Silver Spring, MD.

Bascue, L. O., & Lawrence, R. E. (1977). A study of subjective time and death anxiety in the elderly. *Omega, 8,* 81-90.

Beck, A. T. (1967). Depression: Clinical, experimental and theoretical aspects. New York: Harper & Row.

Bendig, A. W. (1956). The development of the short form of the Manifest Anxiety Scale. *Journal of Consulting Psychology, 20,* 384.

Berman, A. L. (1972). Crisis interventionists and death awareness: An exercise for training in suicide prevention. *Crisis Intervention, 4,* 47-52.

Berman, A. L. (1973). Smoking behavior: How is it related to locus of control, death anxiety, and belief in afterlife. *Omega, 4,* 149-156.

Berman, A. L., & Hays, J. E. (1973). Relationships between death anxiety, belief in afterlife, and locus of control. *Journal of Consulting Psychology, 41,* 318.

Berndt, D. J., Petzel, T., & Berndt, S. M. (1980). Development and initial evaluation of a multiscore depression inventory. *Journal of Personality Assessment, 44,* 4.

Beshai, J. A., & Templer, D. I. (1978). American and Egyptian attitudes toward death. *Essence, 3,* 155-158.

Blakely, K. B. (1975). *Chronic renal failure: A study of death anxiety in dialysis and kidney transplant patients.* Unpublished doctoral dissertation, University of Manitoba, Winnipeg, Manitoba, Canada.

Bluebond-Langner, M. (1978). *The private worlds of dying children.* New Jersey: Princeton University Press.

Bluestone, H., & McGahee, C. (1962). Reaction to extreme stress: Impending death by execution. *American Journal of Psychiatry, 119,* 393-396.

Blythe, B. J. W. (1981). *A comparison among selected groups of day care directors examining their levels of death anxiety and responses to simulated death situations.* Unpublished doctoral dissertation, North Texas State University, Denton, TX.

Bohart, J. B., & Bergland, B. W. (1979). The impact of death and dying counseling groups on death anxiety in college students. *Death Education, 2,* 381-391.

Bolt, M. (1978). Purpose in life and death concerns. *Journal of Genetic Psychology, 132,* 159-160.

Borkeneau, F. (1955). The concept of death. *The 20th Century, 157,* 313–329.

Boulding, K. (1956). *The image.* Ann Arbor, Michigan: University of Michigan Press.

Boyar, J. I. (1964). The construction and partial validation of a scale for the measurement of the fear of death. *Dissertation Abstracts, 25,* 20–21.

Brodksy, B. (1959). The self-representation, anality, and the fear of dying. *Journal of American Psychoanalytic Association, 7,* 95–108.

Bromberg, W., & Schilder, P. (1938). Death and dying. *Psychoanalytic Review, 20,* 133–185.

Bromberg, W., & Schilder, P. (1939). The attitude of psychoneurotics toward death. *Psychoanalytic Review, 23,* 2–25.

Brown, M. B. (1974). *Is there a relationship between death anxiety and purpose in life?* Unpublished doctoral dissertation, University of Ottawa, Ottawa, Ontario, Canada.

Brown, M. C. (1975). *Death confrontation: Does it influence levels of death anxiety and life purpose?* Unpublished doctoral dissertation, University of Ottawa, Ottawa, Ontario, Canada.

Brown, N. O. (1959). *Life against death.* Middletown, CT: Wesleyan University Press.

Brown, O. J. (1977). *Fear of death and western protestant ethic personality traits.* Unpublished doctoral dissertation, Ohio State University, Columbus, OH.

Brown, R. (1983). Locus of control sex role orientation of women graduate students. *College Student Journal, 17,* 10–12.

Bryne, D. (1964). Repression-sensitization as a dimension of personality. In B. A. Maher (Ed.), *Progress in experimental personality research* (pp. 169–220). New York: Academic Press.

Burnett, R. (1982). *Personality factors and circumstances contributing to a woman's response to sexual assault.* Unpublished doctoral dissertation, California School of Professional Psychology at Fresno.

Bushnell, F. K. L. (1982). *Death anxiety among medical-surgical staff nurses as a function of level of nursing education, years of experience, and self-reported comfort while caring for dying patients.* Unpublished doctoral dissertation, Boston University, Boston.

Butler, R. N. (1963). The life review: An interpretation of reminiscence in the aged. *Psychiatry, 26,* 65–76.

Campbell, D. T. (1960). Recommendations for APA test standards regarding construct, trait, or discriminant validity. *American Psychologist, 15,* 546–553.

Cappon, D. (1969). The dying. *Psychiatric Quarterly, 18,* 466–489.

Caprio, F. S. (1950). A study of some psychological reactions during prepubescence to the idea of death. *Psychometric Quarterly, 24,* 495–505.

Caro, J. S., & Campos, F. R. (1980). Miedo y ansiedad ante la muerte. *Revista Espanola de Geriatria y Gerontologia, 15,* 67–80.

Carrera, R. N. (1977). *Implosive scripts.* Unpublished manuscript. (Available from R. N. Carrera, Psychology Department, University of Miami, Coral Gables, Florida.)

Casciani, J. M. (1976). *The relationship between self concept and experimentally induced death anxiety.* University Microfilm International, Washington, D.C.

Cassirer, E. (1953). *An essay on man.* New York: Doubleday Anchor.

Cattell, R. B. (1966). The scree test for the number of factors. *Multivariate Behavioural Research, 2,* 245.

Chandler, A. R. (1950). Attitudes of superior groups toward retirement and old age. *Journal of Gerontology, 6,* 254–261.

Chiapetta, W., Floyd, H. H., Jr., & McSeveney, O. R. (1976). Sex differences in coping with death anxiety. *Psychological Reports, 39,* 945–946.

Choron, J. (1964). *Modern man and morality.* New York: Macmillan.

Christ, A. E. (1961). Attitudes toward death among a group of acute geriatric patients. *Journal of Gerontology, 16,* 56–59.

Cole, M. A. (1978–1979). Sex and marital status differences in death anxiety. *Omega, 9,* 139–147.

Collett, L., & Lester, D. (1969). The fear of death and the fear of dying. *Journal of Psychology, 72,* 179–181.

Cooley, W. W., & Lohnes, P. R. (1962). *Multivariate procedures for the behavioral sciences.* New York: Wiley.

Corey, L. G. (1961). An analogue of resistance to death awareness. *Journal of Gerontology, 16,* 59–60.

Couch, A., & Keniston, K. (1960). Yeasayers and naysayers: Agreeing response set as a personality variable. *Journal of Abnormal and Social Psychology, 60,* 151–174.

Craddick, R. A. (1972). Symbolism of death: Archetypal and personal symbols. International Journal of Symbology, 3, 35–42.

Cronbach, I. J., & Meehl, P. E. (1955). Construct validity in psychological tests. *Psychological Bulletin, 52,* 281–302.

Crowne, D. P., & Marlowe, D. (1960). A new scale of social desirability independent of psychopathology. *Journal of Consulting Psychology, 24,* 349–354.

Cummings, E., & Henry, W. E. (1961). *Growing old: The process of disengagement.* New York: Basic Books.

Curtis, M. J. (1980). *The relationship between bimodal consciousness, meditation and two levels of death anxiety.* Unpublished doctoral dissertation, California School of Professional Psychology, Los Angeles.

Davis, S. F., Martin, D. A., Wilee, C. T., & Voorhees, J. W. (1978). Relationship of fear of death and loss of self esteem in college students. *Psychological Reports, 42,* 419–422.

Denton, J. A., & Wisenbaker, M. (1977). Death experiences and death anxiety among nurses and nursing students. *Nursing Research, 26,* 61–64.

Devins, G. M. (1979). Death anxiety and voluntary passive euthanasia. *Journal of Consulting and Clinical Psychology, 47,* 301–309.

Devins, G. M. (1980–1981). Contributions of health and demographic status to death anxiety and attitudes toward voluntary passive euthanasia. *Omega, 11,* 291–300.

Dickstein, L. S. (1972). Death concerns: Measurement and correlates. *Psychological Reports, 30,* 563–571.

Dickstein, L. S. (1977–1978). Attitudes toward death, anxiety, and social desirability. *Omega, 8,* 369–378.

Dickstein, L. S. (1978). Attitudes toward death, anxiety, and social desirability. *Omega, 30,* 563–572.

Dickstein, L. S., & Blatt, S. J. (1966). Death concern, futurity, and anticipation. *Journal of Consulting Psychology, 30,* 11–17.

Diggory, J. C., & Rothman, D. Z. (1961). Values destroyed by death. *Journal of Abnormal and Social Psychology, 63,* 205–210.

Dixon, R. D., & Kinlaw, B. J. R. (1982–1983). Belief in the existence and nature of life after death: A research note. *Omega, 13,* 287–292.

Dunagin, J. M. (1981). *The relationship between death anxiety, interpersonal trust, and gender.* Unpublished doctoral dissertation, United States International University, San Diego, CA.

Durlak, J. (1972). Relationship between individual attitudes toward life and death. *Journal of Consulting and Clinical Psychology, 38,* 463.

Durlak, J. A. (1973). Relationship between various measures of death concern and fear of death. *Journal of Consulting and Clinical Psychology, 41,* 162.

Durlak, J. A. (1978–1979). Comparison between experimental and didactic methods of death education. *Omega, 9,* 57–66.

Durlak, J. A. (1982). Measurement of the fear of death: An examination of some existing scales. *Journal of Clinical Psychology, 28,* 545–547.

Durlak, J. A., & Kass, C. A. (1981–1982). Clarifying the measurement of death attitudes: A factor analytic evaluation of fifteen self-report death scales. *Omega, 12,* 129–141.

Edwards, M. I. (1983). *The effect of a three-week death education course on the death anxieties of high school sophomores.* Unpublished master's thesis, Mankato State University, Mankato, MN.

Elkins, G. R., & Fee, A. F. (1980). The relationship of physical anxiety to death anxiety and age. *Journal of Genetic Psychology, 137,* 147–148.

Epstein, L. R. (1979). *Death anxiety, repression-sensitization and sensation seeking: Analogue therapist personality variables and their relation to response effectiveness.* Unpublished doctoral dissertation, University of Delaware, Newark, DE.

Erickson, E. (1959). Identity and the life cycle. *Psychological Issues,* Monograph, 1959.

Faunce, W. A., & Fulton, R. L. (1968). The sociology of death: A neglected area of research. *Social Forces, 63,* 205–210.

Feifel, H. (1955). Attitudes of mentally ill patients toward death. *Journal of Nervous and Mental Disorders, 122,* 375–380.

Feifel, H. (1956). Older persons look at death. *Geriatrics, 61,* 127–130.

Feifel, H. (1959). *The meaning of death.* New York: McGraw-Hill.

Feifel, H. (1969). Attitudes toward death: A psychological perspective. *Journal of Consulting and Clinical Psychology, 33,* 292–295.

Feifel, H. (1976). Religious conviction and fear of death among the healthy and terminally ill. In R. Fulton (Ed.), *Death and anxiety* (pp. 131–143). Baltimore: Charles Press.

Feifel, H., & Branscomb, A. B. (1973). Who's afraid of death? *Journal of Abnormal Psychology, 81,* 282–288.

Feifel, H., & Jones, R. B. (1968). Perceptions of death as related to nearness of death. *Proceedings of the 76th Annual Convention of the American Psychological Association, 3,* 545–546.

Fenichel, O. (1945). *The psychoanalytic theory of neurosis.* New York: Norton.

Flint, G. A., Gayton, W. F., & Ozmon, K. L. (1983). Relationship between life satisfaction and acceptance of death by elderly persons. *Psychological Reports, 53,* 290.

Frankl, V. E. (1955). *The doctor and the soul.* New York: Knopf.

Frankl, V. E. (1962). *Man's search for meaning.* Boston, Beacon Press.

Frazier, Sir J. G. (1959). *The new golden bough.* New York: Mentor and Plume Books.

Freud, S. (1909). Notes upon a case of obsessional neurosis. *The standard edition of the complete psychological works of Sigmund Freud,* vol. 10. London: Hogarth Press.

Freud, S. (1918). *Reflections on war and death.* New York: Moffat Yard.

Freud, S. (1920). Beyond the pleasure principle. *The standard edition of the complete psychological works of Sigmund Freud,* vol. 18. London: Hogarth Press.

Freud, S. (1925). The theme of the three caskets. In E. M. Jones (Ed.), *Collected papers,* vol. 14. London: Hogarth Press.

Fromm, E. (1964). *The heart of man.* New York: Harper & Row.

Gibbs, H. W., & Achterberg-Lawles, J. (1978). Spiritual value and death anxiety: Implications for counseling with terminal cancer patients. *Journal of Counseling Psychology, 25,* 563–569.

Gielen, A. C., & Roche, K. A. (1979–1980). Death anxiety and psychometric studies in Huntington's disease. *Omega, 10,* 135–145.

Gilliland, J. (1982). *Death anxiety: Relation to subjective state.* Unpublished doctoral dissertation, California School of Professional Psychology, at Fresno.

Gilliland, J. C., & Templer, D. I. (1985–1986). Relationship of death anxiety scale factors to the subjective state. *Omega, 16,* 155–167.

Gillion, V. E., Jr. (1972). *Victorian cemetery art.* New York: Dover.

Giroux, D. E. (1979). An investigation of the relationship between death anxiety and future orientation, future extension, and time anxiety in senior baccalaureate nursing students. Unpublished doctoral dissertation, New York University, New York, NY.

Gitelson, M. (1948). The emotional problems of elderly people. *Geriatrics, 3,* 135–150.

Goldfried, M., & Davison, G. (1976). *Clinical behavior therapy.* New York: Holt, Rinehart and Winston.

Goldney, R. D. (1981). Attempted suicide in young women: Correlates of lethality. *British Journal of Psychiatry, 139,* 382–390.

Goldsmith, M. D. (1978). *Future health educators and death education.* Unpublished doctoral dissertation. Southern Illinois University at Carbondale.

Golub, S., & Reznikoff, M. (1971). Attitudes toward death: A comparison of nursing students and graduate nurses. *Nursing Research, 2,* 503–508.

Goodman, J. S. (1978). *The transmission of parental trauma: Second generation effects of Nazi concentration camp survival.* Unpublished doctoral dissertation, California School of Professional Psychology, at Fresno.

Gough, H. G. (1953). A non-intellectual intelligence test. *Journal of Consulting Psychology, 17,* 242–255.

Greenberg, H. R., & Blank, E. (1970). Dreams of a dying patient. *Journal of Medical Psychology, 43,* 355–362.

Greenberger, E. (1965). Fantasies of women confronting death. *Journal of Consulting Psychology, 29,* 252–260.

Greyson, B., & Stevenson, I. (1980). The phenomenology of near-death experiences. *American Journal of Psychiatry, 137,* 1193–1196.

Grosser, G. H., Wechsler, H., & Greenblat, M. (1965). *The threat of impending disaster: Contribution to a psychology of stress.* Cambridge, MA: MIT Press.

Hackett, T. P., & Weisman, A. D. (1965). Reactions to the imminence of death. In G. H. Grosser, H. Wechsler, & M. Greenblat (Eds.), *The threat of impending disaster: Contribution to a psychology of stress.* Cambridge, MA: MIT Press.

Handal, P. J. (1969). The relationship between subjective life expectancy, death anxiety, and general anxiety. *Journal of Clinical Psychology, 25,* 39–42.

Handal, P. J., Peal, R. L., Napoli, J. C., & Austrin, H. R. (1984–1985). A relationship between direct and indirect measures of death anxiety. *Omega, 15,* 245–262.

Handal, P. J., & Rychlak, J. F. (1971). Curvilinearity between dream content and death anxiety and the relationship of death anxiety to repression sensitization. *Journal of Abnormal Psychology, 77,* 11–16.

Hardt, D. V. (1978–1979). An investigation of the danger of bereavement. *Omega, 9,* 279–285.

Harlow, J. L. (1976). *The relationship between nurse behavior and attitudes toward terminal patients and nurse exposure to three desensitization experimental conditions.* Unpublished doctoral dissertation, Florida State University, Tallahassee.

Harris, L. (1975). Survey of Attitudes and Perceptions of the Elderly by Various Age Groupings for the National Council on Aging, Washington, D.C.

Hartshore, T. S. (1979). *The grandparent and grandchild relationship and life satisfaction, death anxiety, and attitude toward the future.* Unpublished doctoral dissertation, The University of Texas at Austin.

Heide, F. J., & Borkovec, T. D. (1983). Relaxation-induced anxiety: Paradoxical anxiety enhancement due to relaxation training. *Journal of Consulting and Clinical Psychology, 5*(2), 171–182.

Hinton, J. M. (1963). The physical and mental distress of dying. *Quarterly Journal of Medicine, New Series, 32,* 125.

Hoelter. J. W., & Hoelter, J. A. (1978). The relationship between fear of death and anxiety. *Journal of Psychology, 99,* 225-226.

Hoelter, J. W., & Hoelter, J. A. (1980–1981). On the interrelationships among exposure to death and dying, fear of death and anxiety. *Omega, 11,* 241–254.

Holbein, H. (1971). *The dance of death.* New York: Dover.

Holmes, C. B., & Anderson, D. J. (1980). Comparison of four death anxiety measures. *Psychological Reports, 46,* 1341–1342.

Hunt, D. M., Lester, D., & Ashton, N. (1983). Fear of death, locus of control and occupation. *Psychological Reports, 53,* 1022.

Hutschuecker, A. A. (1959). Personality factors in dying patients. In H. Feifel (Ed.), *The meaning of death.* New York: McGraw-Hill.

Iammarino, N. K. (1975). Relationship between death anxiety and demographic variables. *Psychological Reports, 37,* 262.

Incagnoli, T. (1981). *The relation between locus of control, smoking behavior and death anxiety in a chronic lung population.* Unpublished doctoral dissertation, St. John's University.

Indries, Shah. (1971). *Reflections.* Baltimore, MD: Penguin Books, p. 15.

Jeffers, F. C., Nichols, C. R., & Eisdorfer, C. (1961). Attitudes of older persons toward death. A preliminary review. *Journal of Gerontology, 16,* 53–56.

Johnson, J. C. (1980). Death anxiety of rehabilitation counselors and clients. *Psychological Reports, 46,* 325–326.

Joy, V. L. (1963). Repression-sensitization and interpersonal behavior. Paper read at APA, Philadelphia.

Jung, C. G. (1933). *Modern man in search of a soul.* New York: Harcourt, Brace and World.

Jung, C. G. (1958). *Psyche and symbol.* New York: Doubleday.

Jung, C. G. (1959). The soul and death. In H. Feifel (Ed.), *The meaning of death* (pp. 3–15). New York: McGraw-Hill.

Kahoe, R. O., & Dunn, R. F. (1975). The fear of death and religious attitudes and behavior. *Journal for the Scientific Study of Religion, 14,* 379–382.

Kaiser, H. F. (1967). Program Relate. Mimeo. University of Illinois, Urbana.

Kalinowsky, L. B., & Hoch, P. H. (1952). *Shock treatments, psychosurgery, and other treatments in psychiatry.* New York: Grune and Stratton.

Kalish, R. A. (1963). An approach to the study of death attitudes. *American Behavioral Sciences, 6,* 68–70.

Kane, A. C., & Hogan, J. D. (1985–1986). Death anxiety in physicians: Defensive style, medical specialty, and exposure to death. *Omega, 16,* 11–22.

Kasper, F. E., & Vesper, J. J. (1976). Death anxiety in a risk-taking group. *Essence, 1,* 95–97.

Kastenbaum, R. (1977). *Death, society and human experience.* St. Louis: Mosby.

Kastenbaum, R. (1979). *Between life and death.* New York: Springer.

Kastenbaum, R., & Aisenberg, R. (1972, 1977). *The psychology of death.* New York: Springer.

Kastenbaum, R., & Costa, P. T. (1977). Psychological perspectives on death. *Annual Review of Psychology, 28,* 225–249.

Katz, R. I. (1981). *Death attitudes among heroin addicts.* Unpublished doctoral dissertation, California School of Professional Psychology at Fresno.

Kavanaugh, R. E. (1977). *Facing death.* New York: Penguin Books.

Keller, J. W., Sherry, O., & Piotrowski, C. (1984). Perspectives on death: A developmental study. *Journal of Psychology, 116,* 137–142.

Kelly, P. M. (1979). *An investigation of the concept of Helicy and the effects of aging on reminiscence, life review, life satisfaction, and death anxiety.* Unpublished doctoral dissertation, University of Louisville, KY.

Kelman, H. (1960). Kairos and the therapeutic process. *Journal of Existential Psychiatry, 1,* 233–269.

Kinlaw, B. J. R., & Dixon, R. D. (1980–1981). Fear of death and fertility reconsidered. *Omega, 11,* 119–137.

Kirby, M., & Templer, D. I. (1975). Death anxiety and social work students. Paper presented at the Foundation of Thanatology Symposium. *The family and death: A social work symposium.* New York, NY, April 12, 1975.

Klein, M. (1948). A contribution to the theory of guilt and anxiety. *International Journal of Psychoanalysis, 29,* 114–123.

Klug, L. F., & Boss, M. (1976). Factorial structure of the death concern scale. *Psychological Reports, 38,* 107–112.

Klug, L. F., & Boss, M. (1977). Further study of the validity of the death concern scale. *Psychological Reports, 40,* 907–910.

Koob, P. B., & Davis, S. F. (1977). Fear of death in military officers and their wives. *Psychological Reports, 40,* 261–262.

Koocher, G. P., O'Malley, J. E., Foster, D., & Grogan, J. C. (1976). Death anxiety in normal children and adolescent. *Psychiatria Clinica, 9,* 220–229.

Kopel, K., O'Connell, W., Paris, J., Girardi, P., & Batsel, W. (1977). A human relations laboratory approach to death and dying. *Omega, 6,* 219–221.

Kreiger, S., Epsting, F., & Leitner, L. M. (1974). Personal constructs, threat, and attitudes toward death. *Omega, 5,* 299–310.

Kübler-Ross, E. (1969). *On death and dying.* New York: Macmillan.

Kumar, A., Vaidya, A. K., & Dwivedi, A. V. (1982). Death anxiety as a personality dimension of alcoholics and non-alcoholics. *Psychological Reports, 51,* 634.

Kuperman, S. K., & Golden, S. J. (1978). Personality correlative of attitude toward death. *Journal of Clinical Psychology, 34,* 661–663.

Kurlychek, R. T. (1978–1979). Assessment of attitudes toward death and dying: A critical review of some available methods. *Omega, 9,* 37–47.

Latanner, B., & Hayslip, B. (1984–1985). Occupation-related differences in levels of death anxiety. *Omega, 15,* 53–66.

Laube, J. (1977). Death and dying workshop for nurses: Its effect on their death anxiety level. *International Journal of Nurses Studies, 14,* 111–120.

Lazarus, A. A. (1968). Behavior therapy in groups. In G. M. Gazda (Ed.), *Basic approaches to group psychotherapy and group counseling.* Springfield, IL: Charles C Thomas.

Lefcourt, H. M. (1966). Repression-sensitization: A measure of the evaluation of emotional expression. *Journal of Consulting Psychology, 30,* 444–449.

Lehner, E. (1956). *The picture book of symbols.* New York: William Penn Publishing Corp.

Lessing, G. E. (1769). *Wie die alten den tod gebildet.* Lepizig: Reclam, *4,* 172–221.

Lester, D. (1967a). Experimental and correlational studies of the fear of death. *Psychological Bulletin, 67,* 26–36.

Lester, D. (1967b). Fear of death of suicidal persons. *Psychological Reports, 20,* 1077–1078.

Lester, D. (1970). The need to achieve and the fear of death. *Psychological Reports, 27,* 516.

Lester, D. (1972). Studies in death attitudes: II. *Psychological Reports, 30,* 440.

Lester, D., & Kam, E. (1971). Effects of a friend dying upon attitudes toward death. *Journal of Social Psychology, 83,* 149–150.

Lester, D., & Lester, G. (1970). Fear of death, fear of dying, and threshold differences for death words and neutral words. *Omega, 1,* 175–179.

Lester, D., & Schumacher, J. (1969). Schizophrenia and death concern. *Journal of Projective Techniques and Personality Assessment, 33,* 403–405.

Lester, D., Getty, C., & Kneisl, C. R. (1974). Attitudes of nursing students and nursing faculty toward death. *Nursing Research, 23,* 50–53.

Leviton, D., & Fretz, B. (1978–1979). Effects of death education on fear of death and attitudes towards death and life. *Omega, 9,* 267–277.

Lifton, R. J. (1965). Psychological effects of the atomic bomb in Hiroshima: The theme of death. In G. H. Grosser, H. Wechsler, & M. Greenblat (Eds.), (pp. 152–193). Cambridge, MA: MIT Press.

Lifton, R. J. (1968). Protean man. *Partisan Review, 35,* 13–27.

Lifton, R. J. (1976). The sense of immortality: On death and the Continuity of life. In R. Fulton (Ed.), *Death and identity.* Bowie, MD: Charles Press.

Lifton, R. J. (1979). *The broken connection.* New York: Simon and Shuster.

Lindemann, E. (1944). Symptomatology and management of acute grief. *American Journal of Psychiatry, 101,* 141–148.

Litman, J. M. (1979). *The effect of bereavement on death anxiety, manifest anxiety, and locus of control.* Unpublished doctoral dissertation, University of Missouri, Kansas City.

Lockard, B. E. (1982). *The effectiveness of a death educational instructional unit as an agent of change in the death anxiety level of associate degree nursing students.* Unpublished doctoral dissertation, Mississippi State University.

Loewen, I. L. (1984). Widowhood: The relationship between religious orientation and adjustment to loss of spouse. Doctoral Dissertation. California School of Professional Psychology at Fresno.

Lonetto, R. (1980). *Children's conceptions of death.* New York: Springer.

Lonetto, R. (1982). Personifications of death and death anxiety. *Journal of Personality Assessment, 46,* 404–408.

Lonetto, R., and Templer, D. I. (1983). The nature of death anxiety. In C. D. Spielberger and J. N. Butcher (Eds.), *Advances in personality assessment,* vol. 3. Hillsdale, NJ: Lawrence Erlbaum Associates, pp. 141–174.

Lonetto, R., Fleming, S., & Mercer, G. W. (1979). The structure of death anxiety: A factor analytic study. *Journal of Personality Assessment, 43,* 388–392.

Lonetto, R., Fleming, S., Clare, M., & Gorman, M. (1976). The perceived sex of death and concerns about death. *Essence, 1,* 45–58.

Lonetto, R., Fleming, S., Gorman, M., & Best, S. (1975). The psychology of death:

A course description with some student perceptions. *Ontario Psychologist, 7,* 9–14.
Lonetto, R., Mercer, G. W., Fleming, S., Bunting, B., & Clare, M. (1980). Death anxiety among university students in Northern Ireland and Canada. *Journal of Psychology, 104,* 75–82.
Lowry, R. (1965). *Male-female differences in attitudes toward death.* Unpublished doctoral dissertation, Brandeis University, Waltham, MA.
Lucas, R. A. (1974). A comparative study of measures of general anxiety and death anxiety among three medical groups including patient and wife. *Omega, 5,* 233–243.
Martin, D., & Wrightsman, L. S. (1964). Religion and fears about death: A critical review of research. *Religious Education, 59,* 174–176.
Martin, D., & Wrightsman, L. S. (1965). The relationship between religious behavior and concern about death. *Journal of Social Psychology, 65,* 317–323.
Martin, T. O. (1982–1983). Death anxiety and social desirability among nurses. *Omega, 13,* 51–58.
Mauer, A. (1964). Adolescent attitudes toward death. *Journal of Genetic Psychology, 195,* 75–90.
McClam, P. (1980a). The effects of death education on fear of death and death anxiety among health care and helping professionals. *Dissertation Abstracts International, 39A,* 6548–6549.
McClam, P. (1980b). Death anxiety before and after death education: Negative results. *Psychological Reports, 46,* 513–514.
McClelland, D. (1963). The harlequin complex. In R. White (Ed.), *The study of lives* (pp. 94–119). New York: Atherton Press.
McMordie, W. R. (1978). *Improving the measurement of death anxiety.* Unpublished doctoral dissertation, University of Ottawa, Ottawa, Ontario, Canada.
McMordie, W. R. (1979). Improving measurement of death anxiety. *Psychological Reports, 44,* 975–980.
McMordie, W. R. (1981). Religiosity and fear of death: Strength of belief system. *Psychological Reports, 49,* 921–922.
McMordie, W. R. (1982). Concurrent validity of Templer and Templer/McMordie death anxiety scales. *Psychological Reports, 51,* 264–266.
McMordie, W. R., & Kumar, A. (1984). Cross-cultural research on the Templer and Templer/McMordie death anxiety scales. *Psychological Reports, 54,* 959–963.
McCully, R. S. (1963). Fantasy productions of children with a progressively crippling and fatal disease. *Journal of Genetic Psychology, 102,* 203–216.
McCully, R. S. (1971). *Roschach theory and symbolism: A Jungian approach to clinical material.* Baltimore: Williams & Wilkins.
McDonald, C. W. (1976). Sex, religion, and risk-taking behavior as correlates of death anxiety. *Omega, 7,* 35–44.
McDonald, R. T., & Carroll, J. D. (1981). Three measures of death anxiety: Birth order effects and concurrent validity. *Journal of Clinical Psychology, 37,* 574–577.
McGee, A. Y. (1980). Impact of an educational intervention module on death and

dying on death anxiety among middle-aged and older adults in North Carolina. Doctoral dissertation, North Carolina State Univesity at Raleigh.

Means, M. H. (1936). Fears of 1,000 college students. *Journal of Abnormal and Social Psychology, 31,* 291–311.

Meerloo, J. A. (1955). Transference and resistance in geriatric psychotherapy. *Psychoanalytic Review, 42,* 1.

Meisner, W. W. (1958). Affective response to psychoanalytic death symbols. *Journal of Abnormal and Social Psychology, 56,* 295–299.

Mercer, G. W., & Bunting, B. (1979). Chronic environmental threat and the repression of death-related cognitions. *Essence, 3,* 79–84.

Mercer, G. W., Bunting, B., & Snook, S. (1979). The effects of location, experiences with the civil disturbances and religion on death anxiety and manifest anxiety in a sample of Northern Ireland university students. *British Journal of Social and Clinical Psychology, 18,* 137–145.

Middleton, W. C. (1936). Some reactions toward death among college students. *Journal of Abnormal and Social Psychology, 21,* 165–173.

Minean, J. O., & Brush, L. R. (1980–1981). The correlations of attitudes toward suicide with death anxiety, religiosity, and personal closeness. *Omega, 11,* 317–324.

Morgan, D. W. (1976). Altered states variables as predictors of death anxiety. *Essence, 1,* 34–41.

Morrison, J. K., Vanderwyst, D., Cocozza, J. J., & Dowling, S. (1981–1982). Death concern among mental health workers. *Omega, 12,* 189–208.

Mosher, D. L. (1966). The development and multitrait-multimethod matrix analysis of three measures of three aspects of guilt. *Journal of Consulting Psychology, 30,* 25–29.

Mulholland, R. E. (1980). A comparison of death anxiety among nephrology social workers and social workers in a non-death and dying situation. Unpublished master's dissertation, Catholic University of America, Washington, D.C.

Mulholland, R. E. (1982). Death anxiety in nephrology social workers. *Perspectives, 4,* 114–122.

Murray, P. (1974). Death education and its effect on the death anxiety level of nurses. *Psychological Reports, 35,* 1250.

Myers, J. E., Wass, H., & Murphy, M. (1980). Ethnic differences in death anxiety among the elderly. *Death Education, 4,* 237–244.

Myska, M. J., & Pasework, R. A. (1978). Death attitudes of residential and non-residential rural aged persons. *Psychological Reports, 43,* 1235–1238.

Nagy, M. (1948). The child's theories concerning death. *Journal of Genetic Psychology, 73,* 3–27.

Natterson, J. M., & Knudson, A. G., Jr. (1960). Observations concerning fear of death in fatally ill children and their mothers. *Psychosomatic Medicine, 22,* 456–465.

Nehrke, M. F., Belluci, G., Gabriel, S. J. (1977–1978). Death anxiety, locus of control, and life satisfaction in the elderly: Toward a definition of ego-integrity. *Omega, 8,* 359–368.

Nehrke, M. F., Morganti, J. B., Willrich, R., & Hulicka, I. M. (1979). Health status, room size, and activity level: Research in an institutional setting. *Environment and Behaviour, 11*, 451–463.

Neimeyer, R. A., & Chapman, K. M. (1980–1981). Self/ideal discrepancy and fear of death: The test of an existential hypothesis. *Omega, 11*, 233–240.

Nelson, L. D. (1978). The multidimensional measurement of death attitudes: Construction and validation of a three-factor instrument. *The Psychological Record, 28*, 525–533.

Nelson, L. D., & Nelson, C. C. (1975). A factor analytic inquiry into the multidimensionality of death anxiety. *Omega, 6*, 171–178.

Neufeldt, D. E., & Holmes, C. B. (1979). Relationship between personality traits and fear of death. *Psychological Reports, 45*, 907–910.

Neustadt, W. E. (1982). *Death anxiety in elderly nursing home residents and amount of contact received from staff: A correlation study.* Unpublished master's thesis, University of Oregon, Eugene.

Newman, L. I. (1963). Death: Courage in facing it. In L. I. Newman (Ed.), *The Hasidic anthology.* New York: Schocken.

Nichol, J. (1980). *A study of the effects of a death education unit upon secondary students.* Unpublished doctoral dissertation, Fayetteville, AK.

Nikaya, M. (1961). Asking words of Buddha. In J. Mascaró (Ed.), *The Lamps of Fire*, p. 64. London: Methuen.

North, C. C., & Hatt, P. K. (1947). National opinion research center jobs and occupations: A popular evaluation. *Public Opinion News, 9*, 3–11.

Noyes, R., Jr. (1980). Attitude change following near-death experiences. *Psychiatry, 43*, 234–242.

Noyes, R., Jr. (1981). The encounter with life-threatening danger: Its nature and impact. *Essence, 5*, 21–32.

Nunally, J. (1967). *Psychometric theory.* New York: McGraw-Hill.

Ochs, C. E. (1979). *Death orientation, purpose of life, and the choice of volunteer service.* Unpublished doctoral dissertation, California School of Professional Psychology, at Fresno.

O'Dowd, W. (1984–1985). Locus of control and level of conflict as correlates of immortality orientation. *Omega, 15*, 25–35.

Ohyama, M., Furuta, S., & Hatayama, M. (1978). Death concepts in adolescents. I. Changes of death anxiety in nursing students. *Tohoku Psychologica Folia, 37*, 25–31.

O'Rourke, W. D. (1976). *The relationship between religiousness, purpose-in-life, and fear of death.* Unpublished doctoral dissertation, Boston College, Boston.

Oshman, H. (1978). Death education: An evaluation of programs and techniques. *Catalogue of Selected Documents in Psychology, 8*, 37.

Osipow, S. H., & Grooms, R. R. (1965). Norms for chain of word associations. *Psychological Reports, 16*, 796.

Osis, K. (1961). *Death bed observations by physicians and nurses.* New York: Parapsychology Foundation.

Osis, K., & Haroldsson, E. (1977). *At the hour of death.* New York: Avon.

Pandey, R. E. (1974–1975). Factor analytic study of attitudes toward death amongst college students. *International Journal of Social Psychology, 21*, 7–11.

Pandey, R. E., & Templer, D. I. (1972). Use of Death Anxiety Scale in an inter-racial setting. *Omega, 3,* 127–130.

Paris, J., & Goodstein, L. D. (1966). Responses to death and sex stimulus materials as a function of repression-sensitization. *Psychological Reports, 1966,* 1283–1291.

Parkes, C. M. (1976). The broken heart. In E. Schneidman (Ed.), *Death: Current perspectives,* (pp. 333–346). Palo Alto, CA: Mayfield Publishing Co.

Paul, G. L. (1966). Insight vs Desensitization in Psychotherapy. Stanford, California: Stanford University Press.

Paul, G. L. (1967). Insight vs Desensitization in psychotherapy two years after termination. *Journal of Consulting Psychology, 31,* 333–348.

Peal, R. L., Handal, P. T., & Gilner, F. H. (1981–1982). A group desensitization procedure for the reduction of death anxiety. *Omega, 12,* 61–70.

Penfield, W., & Jasper, H. (1954). *Epilepsy and the functional anatomy of the human brain.* Boston: Little, Brown.

Pepitone-Arreola-Rockwell, F. (1981). Death anxiety: Comparison of psychiatrists, psychologists, suicidologists, and funeral directors. *Psychological Reports, 49,* 979–982.

Pettigrew, C. G., & Dawson, J. C. (1979). Death anxiety: "State" or "trait"? *Journal of Clinical Psychology, 35,* 154–158.

Planansky, K., & Johnston, R. (1977). Preoccupation with death in schizophrenic men. *Journal of Diseases of the Nervous System, 38,* 194–197.

Polderman, R. L. (1976). *An experimental strategy to reduce death anxiety.* Unpublished doctoral dissertation, University of North Carolina at Chapel Hill.

Pollak, J. M. (1977). *Relationship between obsessive personality, death anxiety, and self actualization.* Unpublished doctoral dissertation, Boston College, Boston.

Pollak, J. M. (1979–1980). Correlates of death anxiety: A review of empirical studies. *Omega, 10,* 97–122.

Portz, A. T. (1965). The meaning of death to children. *Dissertation Abstracts, 25,* 7383–7384.

Ramos, F. R. (1982). Personalidad, depresion y muerte. Tesis doctoral, Universidad de Madrid, Madrid, Spain.

Rapaport, D. (1946). *Diagnostic psychological testing, Vol. 2.* Chicago: Yearbook Publishers.

Ray, J. J., & Najman, J. (1974). Death anxiety and death acceptance: A preliminary approach. *Omega, 5,* 311–315.

Redick, R. J. (1975). Behavioral group counseling and death anxiety in student nurses. (Doctoral dissertation, University of Pittsburgh, 1974). *Dissertation Abstracts International, 35,* 1989A (University Microfilms No. 74–20, 809).

Rhudick, P. J., & Dibner, A. S. (1961). Age, personality and health correlates of death concerns in normal aged individuals. *Journal of Gerontology, 16,* 44–49.

Romaniuk, M. (1981). Reminiscence and the second half of life. *Experimental Aging Research,* 7(3):316–336.

Rosenfeld, A. (1966). The vital facts about the drug and its effects. *Life,* March 25, 1966.

Rosenheim, E., & Muchnik, B. (1984–1985). Death concerns in differential levels of consciousness as functions of defense strategy and religious belief. *Omega, 15,* 15–24.

Rosenzweig, S., & Bray, D. (1943). Sibling deaths in the anamneses of schizophrenic patients. *Archives of Neurology and Psychiatry, 49,* 71–92.

Rubenstein, I. (1981). *Multi-generational occurrence of survivor syndrome in the families of holocaust survivors.* Unpublished doctoral dissertation, California School of Professional Psychology, at Fresno.

Ruff, C. F., Ayers, J., & Templer, D. I. (1976). Alcoholism, cigarette smoking, coffee drinking and extroversion. *Journal of Studies on Alcohol, 7,* 983–985.

Ryan, S. M. (1982). *Childhood bereavement: Psychological test findings of a post-death intervention program.* Unpublished doctoral dissertation, University of Minnesota, Duluth.

Sadowski, C. J., Davis, S. F., & Loftus-Vergari, M. C. (1979–1980). Locus of control and death anxiety: A re-examination. *Omega, 10,* 203.

Safier, G. (1964). A study of the relationship between the life and death concepts of children. *Journal of Genetic Psychology, 105,* 283–294.

Salter, C. A., & Salter, C. D. (1976). Attitudes toward aging and behavior toward the elderly among young people as a function of death anxiety. The Gerontologist, 16, 232–236.

Salter, C. A., & Templer, D. I. (1979). Death anxiety as related to helping behavior and vocational interests. *Essence, 3,* 3–8.

Sanders, J. F., Poole, T. E., & Rivero, W. T. (1980). Death anxiety among the elderly. *Psychological Reports, 46,* 53–54.

Sarason, S. B. (1948). Interrelationships among individual difference variables, behavior in psychotherapy and verbal conditioning. *Journal of Abnormal and Social Psychology, 56,* 339–355.

Sarnoff, I., & Corwin, S. M. (1959). Castration anxiety and the fear of death. *Journal of Personality, 27,* 374–385.

Schilder, P. (1936). The attitudes of murderers towards death. *Journal of Abnormal and Social Psychology, 31,* 348–363.

Schilder, P., & Bromberg, W. (1938). Death and dying. *Psychoanalytic Review, 20,* 133–185.

Schilder, P., & Wechsler, D. (1934). The attitudes of children toward death. *Journal of Genetic Psychology, 45,* 406–451.

Schulz, C. M. (1977). Death anxiety and the structuring of a death concerns cognitive domain. *Essence, 1,* 171–188.

Schulz, C. M. (1978). Death anxiety reduction through the success-achievement cultural role value: A middle-class American community case study. *Journal of Psychological Anthropology, 1,* 321–329.

Schulz, R. 1978. *The psychology of death, dying and bereavement.* London: Addison-Wesley.

Schulz, R., & Aderman, D. (1978–1979). Physician's death anxiety and patient outcomes. *Omega, 9,* 327–336.

Schwiebert, D. C. (1978). *Unfavourable stereotyping of the aged as a function of death anxiety, sex, perception of elderly relatives, and a death anxiety repression interaction*. Unpublished doctoral dissertation, Auburn University, Auburn, AL.

Scott, C. A. (1896). Old age and death. *American Journal of Psychology, 8,* 67–122.

Searles, H. F. (1961). Schizophrenia and the inevitability of death. *Psychiatric Quarterly, 36,* 631–665.

Shady, G., Brodsky, M., & Stoley, D. (1979). Validation of the multidimensionality of death anxiety as supported by differences between volunteers and nonvolunteers. *Psychological Reports, 45,* 255–258.

Shepard, S. J. (1980). A study of the relationship between dogmatism and death anxiety, both personal and anticipated from a terminally-ill person, in counseling students, nursing students, and general education students. *Dissertation Abstracts International, 41,* 1411.

Shrut, S. D. (1954). Old age and death attitudes. *Dissertation Abstracts, 16,* 1509–1510.

Shrut, S. D. (1958). Attitudes toward old age and death. *Mental Hygiene, 42,* 259–266.

Shusterman, L. R., & Sechrest, L. (1973). Attitudes of registered nurses towards death in a general hospital. *Psychiatry in Medicine, 4,* 411–426.

Slater, P. E. (1963). *The face of death.* Unpublished manuscript, Cushing Hospital, Framingham, MA.

Slezak, M. E. (1980). *Attitudes toward euthanasia as a function of death fears and demographic variables.* Unpublished doctoral dissertation, California School of Professional Psychology, at Fresno.

Smith, A. H., Jr. (1977). A multivariate study of personality, situational and demographic predictors of death anxiety in college students. *Essence, 1,* 139–146.

Snyder, M., Gertler, R., & Ferneau, E. (1979). Changes in nursing students' attitudes toward death and dying: A measurement of curriculum integration effectiveness. *International Journal of Social Psychology, 19,* 294–298.

Spencer, C. S. (1976). The effect of near-death experience on death anxiety. *Journal of Undergraduate Psychological Research, 3,* 21–26.

Spielberger, C. D., Gorsuch, R. L., and Lushene, R. E. (1970). *Trait anxiety inventory (self-evaluation questionnaire).* Palaupo, CA: Consulting Psychologist Press.

Stacey, C., Chalmers, L., & Markin, K. (1952). The attitude of college students and penitentiary inmates toward death and a future life. *Psychiatric Quarterly Supplement, 26,* 27–32.

Stacey, C. L., & Reichen, M. L. (1954). Attitudes toward death and future life among normal and subnormal adolescent girls. *Exceptional Child, 20,* 259–262.

Stampfl, T. G., & Lewis, D. J. (1967). Essentials of implosive therapy: A learning-theory-based psychodynamic behavioral therapy. *Journal of Abnormal Psychology, 72,* 496–503.

Stern, M. M. (1968). Fear of death and neurosis. *Journal of the American Psychoanalytic Association, 16,* 3–31.

Stevens, S. J., Cooper, P. E., & Thomas, L. E. (1980). Age norms for Templer's Death Anxiety Scale. *Psychological Reports, 46,* 205–206.

Stewart, D. W. (1975). Religious correlates and the fear of death. *Journal of Thanatology, 3,* 161–164.

Stouffer, S. A. (1949). *The American soldier: Combat and its aftermath.* Princeton, NJ: Princeton University Press.

Sullivan, H. S. (1953). *The Interpersonal Theory of Psychiatry.* New York: Norton.

Sullivan, W. J. (1977). *Effect of religious orientation, purpose in life, and locus of control on the death anxiety of college students.* Unpublished doctoral dissertation, Fordham University, New York, NY.

Swenson, W. M. (1961). Attitudes toward death in an aged population. *Journal of Gerontology, 16,* 49–52.

Tarter, R. E., Templer, D. I., & Perley, R. L. (1974). Death anxiety in suicide attempts. *Psychological Reports, 34,* 895–897.

Tate, L. A. (1980). *Life satisfaction and death anxiety in aged women.* Unpublished doctoral dissertation, California School of Professional Psychology, at Fresno.

Taylor, J. A. (1951). The relationship of anxiety to the conditioned eyelid response. *Journal of Experimental Psychology, 41,* 81–92.

Telban, S. G. (1980). *The relationship between death anxiety and the registered nurses' knowledge of the hospice.* Unpublished master's thesis, The Pennsylvania State University, University Park, PA.

Telban, S. G. (1981). Death anxiety and knowledge about death. *Psychological Reports, 49,* 648.

Templer, D. I. (1967). *The construction and validation of a Death Anxiety Scale.* Unpublished doctoral dissertation, University of Kentucky, Lexington, KY.

Templer, D. I. (1969). Death anxiety scale. *Proc. 77th Ann. Conven. Amer. Psychol. Assoc., 4,* 737–738.

Templer, D. I. (1970). The construction and validation of a Death Anxiety Scale. *Journal of General Psychology, 82,* 165–177.

Templer, D. I. (1971a). Death anxiety as related to depression and health of retired persons. *Journal of Gerontology, 4,* 521–523.

Templer, D. I. (1971b). The relationship between verbalized and non-verbalized death anxiety. *Journal of Genetic Psychology, 119,* 211–214.

Templer, D. I. (1971c). Relatively non-technical description of the Death Anxiety Scale. *The Archives of the Foundation of Thanatology, 3,* 91–93.

Templer, D. I. (1972a). Death anxiety: Extroversion, neuroticism, and cigarette smoking. *Omega, 3,* 126–127.

Templer, D. I. (1972b). Death anxiety in religiously involved persons. *Psychological Reports, 31,* 361–362.

Templer, D. I. (1976). Two factor theory of death anxiety: A note. *Essence, 2,* 91–94.

Templer, D. I., & Dotson, E. (1970). Religious correlates of death anxiety. *Psychological Reports, 26,* 895–897.

Templer, D. I., & Lester, D. (1974). An MMPI scale for assessing death anxiety. *Psychological Reports, 34,* 238.

Templer, D. I., & Ruff, C. F. (1975). The relationship between death anxiety and religion in psychiatric patients. *Journal of Thanatology, 3,* 165–168.

Templer, D. I., & Ruff, C. F. (1971). Death anxiety scale means, standard deviations, and embeddings. *Psychological Reports, 29,* 173–174.

Templer, D. I., & Salter, C. A. (1979). Death anxiety and mental ability. *Essence, 3,* 85–90.

Templer, D. I., Lester, D., & Ruff, C. F. (1974). Fear of death and feminity. *Psychological Reports, 35,* 530.

Templer, D. I., Ruff, C. F., & Ayers, J. (1974). Alleviation of high death anxiety with symptomatic treatment of depression. *Psychological Reports, 35,* 216.

Templer, D. I., Ruff, C. F., & Ayers, J. (1976). The death anxiety of those who work in funeral homes. In R. Vanderlyn & J. Pine (Eds.), *Acute grief and the funeral.* Springfield, Illinois: Charles C Thomas.

Templer, D. I., Ruff, C. F., & Franks, C. M. (1971). Death anxiety: Age, sex, and parental resemblance in diverse populations. *Developmental Psychology, 4,* 108.

Templer, D. I., Ruff, C. F., & Simpson, M. (1974). Alleviation of high death anxiety with symptomatic treatment of depression. *Psychological Reports, 35,* 216.

Templer, D. I., Barthlow, V. L., Halcomb, P. H., Ruff, C. F., & Ayers, J. L. (1979). The death anxiety of convicted persons. *Corrective and Social Psychiatry, 25,* 18–25.

Templer, D. I., Veleber, D., Lovito, M., Testa, J. A., & Knippers, C. (1983–1984). The death anxiety of gays. *Omega, 14,* 211–214.

Testa, J. A. (1981). Group systematic desensitization and implosive therapy for death anxiety. *Psychological Reports, 48,* 376–378.

Thomas, B. M. (1978). *Impact of a death laboratory on self-concept, generalized anxiety and death anxiety.* Unpublished doctoral dissertation, North Texas State University, Denton, TX.

Thorson, J. A. (1977). Variation in death anxiety related to college students' sex, major field of study, and certain personality traits. *Psychological Reports, 40,* 857–858.

Tobacyk, J., & Eckstein, D. (1980–1981). Death threat and death concerns in the college student. *Omega, 11,* 139–155.

Tolor, A., & Reznikoff, N. (1967). Relationship between insight, repression-sensitization, internal-external control, and death anxiety. *Journal of Abnormal Psychology, 72,* 426–430.

Torrance, E. F. (1958). Psychological aspects of survival: A survey of the literature. *Human Factors Operations Research Laboratories Report,* No. 35.

Truax, C. B., & Carkhoff, R. R. (1967). *Toward Effective Counseling and Psychotherapy: Training and Practice.* Chicago: Aldine.

Vargo, M. E., & Batsel, W. M. (1981). Relationship between death anxiety and components of the self-actualization process. *Psychological Reports, 48,* 89–90.

Vargo, M. E., & Batsel, W. M. (1984). The reduction of death anxiety: A comparison of didactic, experiental and non-conscious treatment. *British Journal of Medical Psychology, 57,* 333–337.

Vargo, M. E., & Black, W. F. (1984). Psychosocial correlates of death anxiety in a population of medical students. *Psychological Reports, 54,* 737–738.

Wagner, K. D., Lorion, R. P., & Shipley, T. E. (1983). Insomnia and Psychosocial Crisis: Two studies of Erickson's developmental theory. *Journal of Consulting and Clinical Psychology, 51*(4):595–603.

Warren, W. G. (1981–1982). Death threat concern, anxiety, fear, and acceptance in death-involved and "at risk" groups. *Omega, 12,* 359–372.

Warren, W. G., & Chopra, F. M. (1978–1979). Some reliability and validity considerations on Australian data from the Death Anxiety Scale. *Omega, 9,* 293–295.

Watson, J., & Raynor, R. H. (1920). Conditioned emotional reactions. *Journal of Experimental Psychology, 3,* 1–4.

Watts, A. (1975). *Psychotherapy East and West.* New York: Pantheon Books.

Wechsler, I. S. (1958). *A textbook of clinical neurology.* Philadelphia: Saunders.

Weinstein, W. H. (1978). The effects of facilitativeness, age differential, and death anxiety of counseling students of conversational avoidance—death and general. *Dissertation Abstracts International, 39,* 138–139.

Weisman, A. D. (1972). *On dying and denying: A psychiatric study of terminality.* New York: Behavioral Publications.

Welsh, G. S. (1956a). Factor dimensions A and R. In G. S. Welsh and E. G. Dahlstrom (Eds.), *Basic readings in the MMPI in psychology and medicine,* (pp. 265–281). Minneapolis: University of Minnesota Press.

Welsh, G. S. (1956b). An anxiety index and an internalization ratio for the MMPI. In G. S. Welsh and E. G. Dhalstrom (Eds.), *Basic readings in the MMPI in psychology and medicine,* (pp. 298–307). Minneapolis: University of Minnesota Press.

Wesch, J. E. (1971). Self-actualization and the fear of death. *Dissertation Abstract International, 3,* 10–B, 6270–6271.

Whelan, W. M., & Warren, W. M. (1980–1981). A death awareness workshop: Theory application and results. *Omega, 10,* 271–275.

White, P. D., Gilner, F. A., Handal, P. J., & Napoli, J. G. (1983–1984). A behavioural intervention for death anxiety in nurses. *Omega, 14,* 33–42.

Whittenberg, J. L. (1980). *Nurses' anxiety about death and dying patients.* Unpublished master's thesis, University of Rochester, Rochester, NY.

Winter, R. (1982). *The relationship between social interest and death anxiety.* Unpublished master's thesis, Bowie State College, Bowie, MD.

Wittkowski, J., & Baumgartner, I. (1977). Religiositat und einstellung zu tod und sterben bei alten menschen. *Zeitschrift fur Gerontologie, 10,* 61–68.

Wittmaier, B. C. (1979–1980). Some unexcused attitudinal consequences of a short course on death. *Omega, 10,* 271–275.

Wolff, K. (1959). *The biological, sociological, and psychological aspects of aging.* Springfield, IL: Charles C Thomas.

Wolff, K. (1967). Helping elderly patients face the fear of death. *Hospital and Community Psychiatry,* May, 142–144.

Wolman, B. B. (1973). *Dictionary of Behavioral Science.* New York: Van Nostrand Reinhold.

Wolpe, J. (1958). *Psychotherapy by reciprocal inhibition.* Stanford, CA: Stanford University Press.

Wolpe, J. (1973). *The practice of behavior therapy.* 2nd ed. New York: Pergamon.

Worchester, A. (1940). *The care of the aged, the dying and the dead.* Springfield, IL: Charles C Thomas.

Young, M., & Daniels, S. (1980). Born again status as a factor in death anxiety. *Psychological Reports, 47,* 367–370.

Zilboorg, G. (1943). Fear of dying. *Psychoanalytic Quarterly, 12,* 465–475.

Zuehlke, T. E., & Watkins, J. T. (1975). The study of psychotherapy with dying patients: An exploratory study. *Journal of Clinical Psychology, 31,* 729–732.

Zung, W. W. (1965). A self-rating depression scale. *Archives of General Psychiatry, 12,* 63–70.

INDEX